THE INVITATION

Living a Meaningful Death

Ancient Jewish Teachings about Death and Dying
And their Lessons for Enriching and
Deepening the Quality of Living

Miriam Maron, BSN, RN, MA, PhD
and Gershon Winkler, PhD

לזכר נשמות אמינו הצדקניות זכרונן לברכה
שרה שינה מרון
ואסתר רבקה וינקלר

We dedicate this book to our precious mothers, of Blessed Memory:
Sonia Maron and
Esther Rivkah Winkler
who invited us here.
We thank you for
The Invitation

Moskowitz:
"Sam, I heard that Seymour died."

Sam:
"Died shmied -- as long as he's
alive and makes a good living."
-- Old Yiddish Quip

Copyright © 2016 Miriam Maron.

All rights reserved. No part of this book may be reproduced, stored, or transmitted by any means—whether auditory, graphic, mechanical, or electronic—without written permission of both publisher and author, except in the case of brief excerpts used in critical articles and reviews as long as the book title and the authors are accorded due credit. Unauthorized reproduction of any part of this work is illegal and is punishable by law.

Published by Ashina
POB 3931, Thousand Oaks, CA 91359
3102813016
Miriam Maron

ISBN: 978-0-5781-7903-2 (sc)
ISBN: 978-0-5781-8073-1 (e)

Because of the dynamic nature of the Internet, any web addresses or links contained in this book may have changed since publication and may no longer be valid. The views expressed in this work are solely those of the authors and do not necessarily reflect the views of Lulu, Inc. and Lulu, Inc. hereby disclaims any responsibility for them.

Any people depicted in stock imagery provided by Thinkstock are models, and such images are being used for illustrative purposes only. Certain stock imagery © Thinkstock.

Cover Design
by Scott Lewis

Lulu Publishing Services rev. date: 6/29/2016

CONTENTS

Foreword	"Live and Let Go"	vii
Preface	"Portals"	xi
Chapter One	Death and Dying	1
Chapter Two	The Invitation	16
Chapter Three	The Tent of Chosen Time	31
Chapter Four	The Red Cow	51
Chapter Five	Perpetuity	60
Chapter Six	The Ebbing Tide	68
Chapter Seven	The Final Moments	77
Chapter Eight	When the Soul Leaves the Body	86
Chapter Nine	"Bad" Spirits	99
Chapter Ten	The Burial	104
Chapter Eleven	Those Left Behind	110
Chapter Twelve	When Death is Violent	116
Chapter Thirteen	The Kaddish	139
Chapter Fourteen	The Four Sentinels of Night	146

FOREWORD

"Live and Let Go"
By Ryan Aaron Emhoff

> And so does God rescue my soul from passing into the Nothing, and I can then remain ever-aware of my life-ness through the clarity of the Divine Light. Indeed, all these things will God cause to happen with a person, twice, even three times, to bring back their soul from the Nothing toward that light which shines in the Light of the Living. (Job 33:28-30)

Death is certain. One can evade taxes, love, car payments, errands, ex-lovers, work, and even taking care of your health, but the reality is that no matter what happens in between, and no matter what we believe, death is waiting for us at the end of the line. An end may very well be the unifying trait of all of our beginnings. The protracted list of sullen descriptions of death could drone on into perpetuity, but all of that has been said before. What I aim to address is something far more familiar to us than death, something that many tend to grapple with on a regular basis, if not for the duration of their lives. That something is the *fear* of death, and we need not give in to that fear if we retain an open mind and cease to fall prey to the pressures that force us to choose prematurely what we believe about the afterlife.

To some, the idea of eternity is comforting, but to others, it may be terrifying. If our existence is never-ending then how are we supposed to feel when we don't like our existence? What if we are afraid of the pain, and afraid that we will be forced to come back to earth to live another excruciating life? What if the sheer scope of what could be out there scares us? What if we don't want to be part of a "bigger picture"? Even if the supposed afterlife is a beautiful place, it can be difficult to subscribe to the notion that anything is forever when we have been taught our whole lives by experience that change is the only force we can count on.

It would be difficult to completely avoid anxiety about death because, frankly, if we are still alive, death is in our future. I believe this particular anxiety is present for most, no matter what his or her beliefs are. An agnostic may put faith in death, because death is the only medium through which an agnostic will be provided with the necessary proof or disproof of an afterlife. The atheist might grapple with the idea that this is all there is to the universe, and that once they die they will never be a conscious being again. However, we do not need to be bullied by fear in any circumstance. Fear of death squeezes us until we provide an answer for what death is because it is shoved in our faces by our existence. We feel that we need to have a solid belief about the afterlife, and an undying faith in that belief because it is the only question posed to us by the universe that we will be called upon to answer, whether we like it or not.

It is highly unnecessary for anyone to be burdened with choosing a perspective on the afterlife if a belief is not already present. It will come. Do not let a fear of death control your emotions and influence you to either choose a view on death, or hold on to the one you have, if it is not what you feel comfortable with. No person, and no thing, can make you truly believe something you are not willing to believe on that deeper, soul-inspired level. A belief will not be natural if it is a product of fear. Belief is an internal harmony of how you perceive something, and who you are. This harmony cannot be manufactured, purchased, won in the lottery, beaten into your head, or inspired by fear.

When reading about death and dying, one might be likely to dismiss the contributions of a 21-year-old on the subject, as a young man studying at university may not have had enough time to accrue any valuable experience on the matter. Death is, however, a part of my future as much as it is for any other person. The date of my death is unknown and the fact of my death is certain, as is the case for anyone of any age.

As it so happens, I have had a fair share of exposure to death. Along the way, both my experiences and my developing sense of self have molded a view on death, and a perspective on the interpretation of death, that I believe has a great power to reduce the fear and anxiety of those who are struggling with their own view on death, or lack thereof. I am not going to try and convince you of anything as I have no interest in converting others to my point of view, but I do have a vested interest in sharing my thoughts on death if they go some distance in staving off fear and anxiety about death for others.

I have lost most of my grandparents, many uncles, other indirect relations, family friends, and a childhood friend. This loss does not make me unique; in fact, I presume it makes me rather average. My point is that I am no stranger to receiving that terrible news, and no stranger to the pain left in its wake. The mere existence of my family is only possible because a small portion of my relatives survived the pandemic of horror and death that was the Holocaust. Many did not. I grew up deeply sobered by my family's past, and how they managed to survive. At the same time I felt I owed it to the dead to remember them, and learn about the lives they *did* have, however brief. I still feel this way, and to me there is nothing more humbling than the moments I have spent in silence recounting their names, and sending them love.

The death of my grandmother is still fresh in my mind. I was honored to help carry her casket, and as I did so I was reminded of how personal the experience was. At that moment, it was just she and I. Everything else seemed to fade away because it was my time with her, my time to grieve and notice that relationship I had with her. There was a part of her passing that was my own to live with. I found solace in the Jewish rituals associated with death. Even though the wound of loss was gaping for those closest to her, the rite of sitting *shiva*, and the incantation of the *Kaddish* seemed to provide a small refuge, something to cling to, in the daily struggle to keep afloat while drifting in the vast loneliness of despair. Her death brought people together to support one another, and it was in this process of mending that I saw the power death has to bring newness. It is this gift of newness of perspective that I find an invaluable upside to terrible loss.

Let it come. That is my simple message. All you can do is be open to what will come because your experiences in life, and your developing sense of self, will both play a role in who you become. If who you are is someone who is not ready to entertain a serious conversation about death, then do not force it. It will not work, and that lack of synchronicity will tear you apart inside if you make yourself subscribe to a belief simply because you think you have to. Even if you feel confident about your perspective on the afterlife, it can still be a good practice to step back from time to time and let the universe reaffirm that view. You never know what will trigger that "aha" moment from the most trying of years, to the silliest of random and seemingly insignificant few seconds. Be open with yourself because it is a balance of intrinsic and extrinsic forces in the universe that coalesce under our supervision to shape our perception of life and death.

It takes a lot of strength to let go of something that causes us so much anxiety, but the payoff is huge. No matter what you believe about death, it is my humble opinion that we should all still pursue loving and helping one another, the cultivation of our relationships, growth, success, and making our dreams realities. In that case, why should it matter what you believe about death when living is the task before you? You should live your life the same way no matter what you believe. Stop defining who you are by how you believe you will experience death because deep within us we know what kind of person we want to be regardless. Listen to that inner voice and chase your dreams without the tethers of death holding you back.

Live and let go.

PREFACE

"Portals"
By Rabbi Dr. Miriam Maron

Compassion, Understanding, Empathy, Love. This is what I offer you and this is what I hope for you. We have all lost. We all grieve. We all walk through this life with a part of us that will never be the same, albeit with varying circumstances that are sometimes extreme; a part of us that we cannot describe in the world of language but that we carry nonetheless. We walk on, and sometimes we need to stop, to acknowledge, allow healing in. Thank you for walking with us as we explore, pause, deepen, expand, contract and embrace.

Ever since I was a young child, I have been keenly aware of Death. I would find myself drawn to movies and books that contained death or dying. And each time, instead of turning me away, they drew me in and only kindled my curiosity further. I would wonder, for example, why those pronounced dead would have their arms placed over their waist with their fingers intertwined so that they had their hands perfectly folded over their body. I remember seeing a Disney display of *Sleeping Beauty* with her hands folded in a similar fashion, and how that image wedged itself firmly in my young mind. As hard as she tried, my mother was unable to distract me from this image, and I kept repeating to myself over and over again, like a mantra: "Sleeping Beauty, Sleeping Beauty." And it made me wonder why she was deemed so especially beautiful, specifically while in this unusually deep state of sleep? Moreover, why would something so beautiful as this deep state of sleep be yet something to fear? As a young girl, then, I wondered why everyone seemed so terrified of such a state of being when the body looked so peaceful, so very much at peace, when the soul journeyed on.

As a daughter of Holocaust Survivors, the remembrance of death loomed ever-present in our home, and the perpetuity of living a constant drive. One trying moment of my childhood was witnessing my father cry while looking at pictures of his parents, his first wife, and the children they shared, all of whom were murdered during World War Two while he was away fighting in the Polish underground. I would never meet my brother and sister from that era, or my paternal grandparents and numerous other relatives on both sides of the family. I would only know them from many moments of taking in their presence from a few photographs. Witnessing my father's pain over his tragic loss, and my mother's grief over losing family as well, contributed significantly to the empathy I already felt for others, and perhaps the courage I find within myself to walk with those who face death or with those who have lost loved ones and are in the process of mourning. Understandably, living but one generation's distance from a momentous genocidal attempt, and with parents who actually survived it, was difficult for me as a young child; difficult to take in the enormity of such pain and such grief. Yet, along with the challenges it brought I am grateful for what I have learned through the process.

Life, death and all of their challenges have always been the focus of my work as an adult. Some people seem to find it hard to understand why I volunteer to be at the bedside of those who are transitioning; why at a young age I chose to do Hospice training and walk hand-in-hand with souls who were facing the unknown next step that so many fear and try to avoid at all costs.

I recall how as a young mother of two (one of whom was still an infant and still being breastfed at the time) I had my hands quite full. I had been continuing my studies in the mystical tradition of our people, known as *Kabbalah*, throughout my pregnancies, and felt the openings of the worlds, one of which was having had the honor of giving birth. I felt compelled to give of myself in the work of *bikkur cholim*. This phrase is often translated as "visiting the sick," which is powerful enough in that it conveys the importance of visiting those in need, whether sick or dying. If we look at the meaning of these words on a deeper level, they also translate as "Discerning the Dreams," as in exploring the imagery that is conjured by our encounter with illness or our approach toward death. In the Judaic Shamanic Wisdom path, it is then not solely about visiting the sick, but also visiting the sickness as well. In my private healing work that is very much the approach I work with. Both I and my client gently embark upon a journey where we dream together, visit the issue together, explore the wisdom of the imagery we both encounter. No one should be alone in illness, dying, mourning, let alone life's challenges. This is the essence of *bikkur cholim*, and it is often a walk in realms beyond, across the threshold of portals otherwise inaccessible.

My introduction to complementary modes of healing ironically began because of an experience I had while I was working as a Registered Nurse on an ENT (Ear Nose Throat) unit in a well-known hospital in Philadelphia, Pennsylvania. One day, during my rounds, I was shocked as I witnessed a patient smoking a cigarette in the lounge through his tracheostomy (an opening surgically created through the neck into the trachea, A.K.A. the windpipe). This man had cancer from years of smoking and had just undergone surgery only a few days earlier. I realized at that moment that as a health practitioner in my position I could not reach people early enough. I wanted to spend more time with patients and have plenty of time to make a heart to heart connection. I decided then and there to pursue *preventive* medicine and entered a graduate program in exercise physiology at the University of Southern California. This process was very rewarding for me, and fit well with my desire to help people live a healthier life, rather than focus on treating them solely physically without time to address other aspects and levels of their path. Around the same time, I also started a practice working with both individuals and corporations to create various training programs and exercise prescriptions. It was wonderful, and yet I yearned to help people explore deeper aspects of their soul-selves. That opportunity came while studying spirituality and mysticism with several spiritual teachers, including Rabbi Jonathan Omer-man, at Metivta: A Center for Contemplative Judaism, based in Los Angeles. At the time, Metivta also served as a healing center and I volunteered for its program of outreach to those who were ill. I found this work to be very fulfilling and also led the chanting and singing for the *Bikkur Cholim Support Group*. We would meet regularly to share experiences, brainstorm regarding any impediments in our visits, and offer emotional and spiritual support as well as inspiration for each other.

One afternoon, I received a call through Metivta and was asked to visit a woman who was very ill and comatose. I was particularly busy that week with numerous family and professional obligations, and my first reaction was to ask for someone else to make the visit. While the phone was still in my hand, I searched my soul and knew there was a deeper reason I was being asked, so I accepted the request.

While on the way to visit "Sharon," I was listening to a *niggun* (wordless melody) that I hadn't heard before. I began to sing along and learn this *niggun* while praying for guidance on how to bring Sharon comfort and healing.

When I arrived at the Intensive Care Unit, I paused to meditate, clearing my mind in preparation for the visit. As I entered the room, I felt a thickness in the air. Sharon was in a coma. She lay in a fetal position with her limbs tightly contracted. She was connected to life-sustaining and monitoring equipment. Seeing this precious person with all the equipment around her and connected to her, I felt a seclusion of body from soul. My reverse isolation gown, mask and gloves might have further created barriers in a physical sense, but only if I allowed it. I put my gloved hand on her delicate arm and within moments, I felt compelled to sing to her. I received this guidance and began to sing various prayers, Yiddish lullabies, and the *niggun* that I had just learned while driving to the hospital.

Soon after I had begun to sing, I was shocked to see this lovely lady open her eyes, slowly turn her head and look deeply into my eyes. It was as though our souls joined in that moment. I will never forget the boundless soul-to-soul connection that I felt. She then began to tear and tried to open her mouth in an attempt to speak, sing or cry out, but she was intubated (an endotracheal tube inserted through the mouth and into her trachea for mechanical ventilation). Actually, Sharon did not need to use words, she communicated from a much deeper place than words: her heart, her soul. I felt a great shift occur for both of us.

As I looked into her eyes, I saw angels surrounding her soul. At that moment she looked into my eyes and I was given the gift of being able to join with her and her ancestors. Life would never be the same after this moment in time, and, in fact, it never was. In those moments, my vision opened as my experience of multidimensional space expanded. I gained a deeper understanding of what my soul's purpose was during my sojourn here on Earth, but without a doubt most important was showing up and being present to help someone in a time of great need.

I continued to visit Sharon in the days that followed. During those visits, I sang again and the response was the same each time, yet with a little less energy as she was slowly transitioning to the next world. At one of the visits she moved deeper into transition. Music is usually wonderful for this stage, but on that particular day I needed to be with her in silent prayer instead. As I spoke to her softly of the World-to-Come and of angels, one of her monitors sounded an alarm. Sharon's nurse rushed into the room, the alarm was quickly silenced and the nurse left. I continued the visit, reminding her that she could feel free to go whenever she was ready. I said good-bye, knowing it would be the last time, and I left for home. I was a witness. I beheld a sacred journey. It was an honor. I felt humbled. I felt immense gratitude. I felt awe. I felt Divine connection!

That night, I was suddenly awakened at 3:00 A.M. My body just sat right up and I felt her presence. The next morning I called the hospital and was told that Sharon had passed at 3:00 A.M. The call confirmed what I had sensed. A soul partner had left this plane of existence. I was so happy she was out of pain, and, at the same time, I was in mourning. Our relationship was so deep, beyond words, beyond worlds.

Later that day, I scheduled an appointment with a body worker. I had worked with this practitioner for many years, but this was the first time I had ever heard him **hum** during a session. As I listened to his humming, it struck me that he was humming the very same *niggun* that became Sharon's, the one I had learned just before my first visit with her; he was humming the same exact tune I had sung to Sharon over and over again during each visit. I was of course surprised and asked if he knew this melody. He shrugged and said he didn't know it at all, actually – "it just came" to him.

Needless to say, I broke out in tears, knowing that Sharon was reaching out to me from beyond. I felt she was now bridging the worlds for me, and I knew beyond a shadow of a doubt that my life had continued to shift. And in fact, my life has become deeper and richer ever since this very powerful experience.

Following this and other enlightening experiences, I began a "music and healing" group with the goal of bringing music to the bedside. It eventually evolved into a workshop called "Healing through Sacred Song and Movement," which provided people with a safe place to explore their own healing processes, a practice I have since incorporated into my current workshops and programs as well as my private healing sessions.

Many years have since passed. At this point in my journey, it gladdens me to work at guiding, motivating, teaching and inspiring as many as I can through their life journeys as I hold them in Divine love. I work to thereby act as a guide through life's bumps, life's transitions and celebrations, while acting as the guardian of the soul. In addition, it is my pleasure and my privilege to assist others in finding their specific purpose as they walk the path of self-exploration, and to help them discover their passions and their dreams. This book is a vital part of that endeavor, as living and dying is a sacred intersection -- a very powerful place of healing -- where precious opportunities lay dormant, waiting for us to accept their invitation to engage in life-shifting adventures.

It has always puzzled me that we celebrate our "birth" days, which are the days when we died from another world and were birthed into this one. Yet when "*yartzeits*" come around, the anniversary of the death of a loved one, we tend not to throw parties. In fact as that anniversary date approaches, we often have a "charge" in our being that can sometimes feel like fear or even dread. Listen to the wisdom of our ancestors:

> It is written in the Scriptures of Solomon: "A good name is better than good oil; and the day of death is better than the day of

birth" (Ecclesiastes 7:1). Said Rabbi Pin'chas: "When Man is born, he is already designated for Death; when he dies he is already designated for Life. When Man is born, everyone rejoices; when he dies, everyone weeps. And it ought not to be so, but rather when a person is born they ought not to rejoice and when he dies they ought to celebrate in that he has departed bearing a good name and has left the world in peace. It is likened onto two boats anchored off on the great sea. One was entering port and one was leaving port. The people gathered to see the outgoing boat were cheering and rejoicing, while the people gathered to greet the incoming boat were silent and solemn. There was a wise man present who then declared, 'I see it the other way around, that you who are cheering and rejoicing for the boat setting off to sea ought to be weeping and grieving, while you who are silent and solemn in response to your boat arriving at port ought to be rejoicing and celebrating. After all, the boat just beginning its journey, its fate is unknown to us and we do not know what ills might befall it, what storms might threaten it, whereas the boat that is arriving, how happy we are that this journey is over and the passengers thereon have returned in peace'" (*Midrash Kohelet Rabbah* 7:4).

Our souls (having come from the place of infinity) may be able to connect to the above teaching more easily, yet our hearts may not always "feel" it in this way, and our minds may continue to question. Perspectives like this may become more accessible to the heart place and to the intellect after you have read this book and some of the deep teachings we have imparted.

I will gladly share with you a method I discovered to be extremely helpful for me. When both of my parents passed on, I found myself struggling greatly with the fact that both of them had passed within a few days of each other (in different years) which also happened to be very close to the date of my birth. To help me figure this out, I used some techniques of *Gematria* (the wisdom of Hebraic Numerology). Without going into great detail, I worked with the respective Hebraic years of their passing and my own birth year, as well as with the days of their passing and my birth **day**, followed by translating the resulting numbers into their Hebrew letter equivalents. I then played with the juxtaposition of the lettering until they formed actual Hebrew words, and discovered some fascinating things. Working with the days of their passing and my birth added up to a number in which the Hebrew equivalent spelled the word מז *maz*, which is a Hebrew/Aramaic word for "soft," which, in turn, softened my heartache. This was a large undertaking as I was still in the first year of mourning at the time, and I wanted to explore this in greater depth. So I asked for the support of Gershon, and, working together through this process, we combined **all** the numbers and watched them lead us to this beautiful combination of letters and words, translated into English as follows:

> "And I have a vision. This is it and it is this. That they shall then come. Behold! Mother of Blood and of Life! And then shall come **The** Mother to bring soft fruition of potential into a beautiful shape and form."

And this poetry softened my struggle, while transmuting another layer of the difficult "charge" I felt in my gut around a particular segment of time in the calendar year which in turn opened me enough to be able to receive The Gift.

Deep struggle in life is true for many, if not for most of us, regardless of whether we have experienced a world at war, its aftermath, everyday demands, or other serious life and death issues we have had to face. I know I am not unique in this. My heart is wide open and extending itself to all of you; all of you who have felt the pain of life as we know it, and death as we tend to perceive it. My hope is that you will find a bit of comfort here. I offer you understanding, love, tools, and a hefty dose of courage to walk the journey of life which, as you will learn in these pages, is also a journey of death. For, as we will explore in more detail throughout this book, we are experiencing in every moment death within life. This is the *good* news!! Our life is in fact a practice, in and of itself, of death! And it gets better. If in every moment of life we are experiencing death, then we are also experiencing birth and renewal in every moment, in every breath. As such, we have the opportunity to let go of that which impedes us in being fully in life, and to truly have ever fresh beginnings. It sounds simple, but it's not easy. With practice, it gets much, much easier as we glimpse the possibilities, and with time we become more and more confident as we feel and experience the results of our efforts, and as we learn how very definitely capable we are.

Both Life and Death are very complicated issues, and to even attempt to be able to cover all possibilities or situations of either would mean the book would never be completed, never finished, never ready for publication.

The process of grieving, too, is a complex one to write about. It is so very individual, dependent upon the person going through the process and their history as well as the type of relationship they had with the deceased. And, very importantly, the circumstances surrounding the deceased person's life and death are also important factors in how we deal with grieving, whether our own or someone else's. The ramifications of a loved one no longer walking the planet in physical form affects the dynamics of family, friends, and relationships in general. All of this needs to be considered.

The more unusual or questionable are circumstances surrounding a death, the more complicated is the process of letting go and the eventual return to the place of celebrating life and living. Being sensitive to the pacing of each and every individual in their process is therefore crucial. For some it may be a year, but for others it may be a journey for the rest of their life. Please be kind to yourself and to others. We all have wounds that are healing at different paces and in different ways. It is not about who heals better or faster! No one truly knows all the circumstances of another no matter how close they may be to them. Some of it is difficult to even put into words and some of it may be too painful to discuss over a cup of coffee. The waves of grief wash over us unexpectedly, sometimes with tears, sometimes with thoughts or a certain sad or empty look.

In the use of any book or ideology or principle or philosophy it is important not to impose any one concept of what is "right" or traditional regarding grieving or the ceremonies/rituals around one who has passed. Within the realm of death and dying we are called to consider both the sensitivity of the bereaved as well as the wishes of the deceased. This is a practice of what it truly means to step aside and think of other, and an enormous challenge. There is no more sensitive a time such as when a death has occurred, for emotions are riding high and the details of the moment can be overwhelmingly daunting, from logistics to rituals.

To those struggling with grief over a loss, I encourage you to honor your very individual personal needs, emotional and otherwise, and grieve in a way that feels congruent with your core beliefs, and feelings, and to do so with ritual and ceremony that support this. At times, your own prayer or ritual needs or desires may differ from those "prescribed" by your community, in which case please honor this and implement them in a separate space. This can be done on your own or with a group of others who will support you in your process.

May the teachings in these chapters allow you to let go of your fear of death which will in turn allow you to let go of your fear in and of life. When you do this you are free to live life fully and therefore free to know and embrace true joy and passion. You have the strength to open this door. How do you begin? I invite you to begin by turning page after page. Each page is a doorway, and when you begin to read, you take the steps to cross the threshold. Clear the space within to allow for the new. Notice your thoughts and wrestle if you'd like. Know your truth and see the connection to universal truth. Explore your feelings. Allow quiet time to integrate. Possibly share your discoveries with someone you feel will be able to meet you in this sacred space. Delight in the fact that you have accepted The Invitation!

May the Divine Wings of Light wrap around you and hold you always. May you feel loved, safe, comforted and supported in all that you are. May the Holy One of Blessing give strength and wisdom to us all, that we may be a beautiful vessel of healing for ourselves and for others. I open my heart and bless you with the light and love of the universe.

CHAPTER ONE

Death and Dying

> It is not in our power to transport the beyond to become here; but we can transport the here to the beyond.[1]

This book attempts to bring together some of the most important teachings about death and dying that have emerged from more than four thousand years of Jewish life wisdom, both in its written and oral traditions. These teachings offer precious guidance for more meaningful **living** as well, and perceive life and death as mutual partners in the infinite cycling and re-cycling of our mysterious existence, each preparing us for the other -- life for death, death for life. The more we come to understand the meaning of death, the better equipped we will be for understanding the meaning of life. After all, the moment we are born, we are already well on our way toward death. Right now, in this very moment that you are reading these words, you are dying. What you choose to **do** with these moments of living that are slipping through your fingers will determine the quality of that process we glibly refer to as death, but which is actually an integral part of living, and, more importantly, part of a series of phases in the ever-unfolding drama of the mystery of existence itself.

The human's obsession with death and dying has led to much lore and mythology, and to as many religious creeds. It is, after all, one of the greatest mysteries of life itself. From the genesis of human history to

---
[1] Abraham Joshua Heschel in *Man is not Alone*, p. 131

this very day, we have not only **feared** death, we have **revered** it, lived in constant **awe** of it, and in some instances given it more credence and respect than life. We have invested far more in dying than in living; spending more to be buried than, say, a life-nurturing vacation, or than we would donate to the living poor. We desperately seek newer ways of extending life and reversing aging, and we pride ourselves in our ability to cheat death with newer and better medications, surgical procedures, organ transplants, and machines that forcibly keep us alive – anything to counter this dreaded phenomenon we call Death. Then there are the countless cultural taboos surrounding death, as well as religious injunctions dictating extent of time prior to burial, whether cremation is prohibited or mandatory, and whether suicide – assisted or otherwise -- is moral or not.

Our intrinsic fear of death stems from our desperate fixation with life, specifically with **staying** alive. There are those who will argue that our fear of death is more about fear of the unknown, of not knowing what will happen to us **after** we die. Actually, they are both one and the same theory. Concern over what happens to us after we die implies a presumption that there is some form of **life** after death, which brings us back to our obsession with staying alive, whether before or after we "die." Naturally, then, we are inclined to wonder, ponder, and imagine wide varieties of possible scenarios of what life would be like on the other side of death. And in so doing, death becomes a tad less dreadful since it is rendered not as The End, but as a transition from one form of life into another. The imbalance in all of this is not so much our meager attempts at trying to figure out what we cannot know for certain, but rather our fixation on life **after** death to the neglect of life **before** death; our fixation on death and dying tomorrow to the neglect of life and living today.

> It is an important fact, however, that unlike other Oriental religions, where the preoccupation with death was the central issue of religious thinking, the Bible rarely deals with death as a problem. There is no rebellion against death, no bitterness over its sting, no preoccupation with the afterlife. In striking contrast

to its two great neighboring civilizations, Egypt with its intense preoccupation with the afterlife and Babylonia with the epic of Gilgamesh, who wanders in search of immortal life, the story of the descent of Ishtar, and the legend of Nergal an Ereshkigal, the Bible is reticent in speaking about these issues. The Hebrew Bible calls for concern for the problem of living rather than the problem of dying. Its central concern is not, as in the Gilgamesh epic, how to escape death but, rather, how to sanctify life.[2]

As a strictly life-affirming spirit path, the Judaic tradition at its core pays astonishingly little attention to what happens **after** we die, focusing instead primarily on what we need to be doing or not doing while we're yet alive. Throughout the written sacred scriptures of the Jews one would go virtually blind reading between the lines to glean so much as crumbs of writ that might only **possibly** allude to the afterlife, almost as if the ancient Jews did not possess any such belief whatsoever. On initial examination, one would come away with the postulate that Jewish belief in the afterlife -- which over the last several millennia became an essential component of the Jewish faith -- must have been borrowed from other cultures following serial invasions of ancient Israel by Philistia, Phoenicia, Babylon, Persia, Greece, Egypt, Assyria, Rome, etc.

In the oldest and most important Hebraic scriptural writ, upon which all subsequent Hebrew scripture and oral tradition is founded -- the תורה Torah, [literally: "Guide"] -- we find only vague suggestion of the afterlife when the Torah describes the act of dying as being: "gathered onto one's people."[3] If this terminology merely connotes burial in a tribal cemetery, it would relieve us of having to explore the issue any further. But often the people about whom this was said died and were buried miles away from the land of their people. We are then left with the probability that such terminology does indeed hint to an extant belief back then in the afterlife. And because the Torah is a Guide

---

[2] Rabbi Abraham Joshua Heschel in *Moral Grandeur and Spiritual Audacity* (Noonday Press), p. 369
[3] Genesis 25:8 and 17; 35:29; 49:33; Numbers 20:24; Deuteronomy 32:50

for the Living,[4] it steers clear of any further elaboration of what happens after death other than a reunion with our families, tribe, and ancestors. In fact, cemeteries did not exist in Jewish tradition before the Jews were exiled to other lands where either they were **forced** to be buried together by host cultures who were unfriendly to Jews, and therefore did not want Jews buried alongside their own, or because Jews, as a tribal people, preferred to be buried together. In ancient Israel, however, you were either buried where you died, or in catacombs beneath the earth, or in caves atop mountains; and if you were a noted teacher, you were buried where you taught most. Visiting Israel today, one will not find ancient cemeteries; one will instead find individual tombs and burial sites scattered across the land on hilltops, or in caves. Originally, the tradition was to bury the dead in the earth and then exhume their bones at a later date to be reburied, or stacked, in cavernous crypts elsewhere.[5] In the Galilee, they would often plant a seed in the mouth of the deceased, usually a prominent spiritual teacher, from which a tree would eventually emerge. One can see this today in Israel when visiting some of the burial sites of the ancient Galilean rabbis, most notably that of the first-century Rabbi Tar'fon who is buried on a hill in a remote region known as Ketitah, with a healthy 2,000-year old tree growing out of his tomb. Bedfellows were buried together in accordance with the third-century Rabbi Yehudah's dictum: "All who slept with him during his life, are buried with him in his death."[6]

While ancient Jewish scriptural writ practically avoids any discussion of the afterlife, it spares no verbiage in discussing **resurrection** of the dead. We find such concepts nonchalantly mentioned in the stories of the Hebrew prophets Elijah, Elisha, Ezekiel, and Daniel.[7] More such accounts appear in the later narratives of the Talmud as well. For example, the second-century Rabbi Chananyah bar Hachino'i who resurrected his wife,[8] Rabbi Pinchas ben Ya'ir who resurrected a girl

---

[4] Leviticus 18:5 and Deuteronomy 30:19
[5] *Talmud Bavli, Ey'vel Rabati,* Ch. 12
[6] *Talmud Bavli, Ey'vel Rabati,* Ch. 13
[7] First Kings 17:22; Second Kings 4:32-25; Isaiah 26:19; Ezekiel 37:12; Daniel 12:2
[8] *Talmud Bav'li, Ketuvot* 62b

who had drowned,⁹ and other such stories of the miraculous powers of the ancient Hebrew sages:

> It happened once that -- due to his poor eyesight – Rabbi Yochanan presumed that Rabbi Kahana was laughing at him (he actually had a cleft lip from an earlier accident). When Rabbi Kahana realized he had inadvertently hurt Rabbi Yochanan's feelings, he became ill and eventually died. Later, when Yochanan was told that Kahana had a cleft lip, and thus he had not at all been laughing at him, Yochanan went to the cave where Kahana was buried so that he might resurrect him. A snake blocked his path at the cave, its tail in its mouth. "I have come to see my colleague," he said to the snake, but the snake wouldn't open its mouth to uncurl, meaning that it would not allow Yochanan to pass. "I've come to see my **friend**, then," but the snake remained in place with tail in mouth. "I've come to see my **master**!" and the snake opened its mouth, released its tail end, and let Yochanan pass. He then resurrected Kahana and bid him to follow him to the House of Study, to which Kahana replied: "Only if you promise not to be so over-sensitive lest I die again and you have to bring me back from the dead yet a **second** time! That would be very hard on me."¹⁰

> Rabbi Yosef the son of Rabbi Yehoshua ben Ley'vee fell ill and died. His father resurrected him, he asked him: "What did you see?" He replied: "I saw the world turned upside down; that which was above was below, and that which was below was above." Said he: "No, my son, you saw the world clearly as it is; for as we are below, so we are above."¹¹

Yet, the resurrections described in these accounts occurred in the land of the living and give us no clue regarding ancient Jewish belief in the afterlife. Only one story in the Hebrew scriptures gives us a glimpse at the possibility that such a belief existed amongst the Jews of antiquity as part of their own cosmology: the account of the tenth-century,

---

⁹ *Midrash Devarim Rabbah* 3:3
¹⁰ *Talmud Bav'li, Baba Kama* 117a-b
¹¹ *Talmud Bav'li, Pesachim* 50a

B.C.E. Hebrew chieftain Saul and his visit with the sorceress of *Eyn Dor* whom he consulted for the purpose of conjuring the spirit of his dead mentor Samuel the Prophet. Although this narrative does not appear in the earlier writ of the Torah, it is still a story dating back to early pre-exilic times when the Hebrews had their own commonwealth, had not been conquered yet by other nations, and were living in their own ancestral homeland as a distinct tribal society. If belief in life-after-death was not on the menu of the ancient Jewish belief system, Saul would never have entertained the notion of calling upon his dead mentor for guidance, nor would the Hebrew scriptural narrative have recorded the story, or at least not affirmed that the séance worked and that the dead prophet actually ended up communicating with the living chieftain. But it did.[12]

In fact, in examining the subsequent writ of Solomon the Wise (10th-century B.C.E.), one finds that Solomon did not position Death on the opposite side of Life but on the opposite side of **Birth**.[13] Life was not seen as a **contrast** to Death. Rather, Solomon taught, Life always was, and always is, and always will be. In the commentative writings of the second-century school of Rabbi Tanchuma (which appears in a later chapter) this becomes more clear in his depiction of birth and death as actually the same process, albeit our **experience** of each is different.[14] When we are born into this life realm, in other words, we are born by virtue of having died in a previous life realm, and when we die in this life realm, we are born into yet another life realm by virtue of having died in this one. As the second-century Rabbi El'azar HaKafar put it: "The newborns are for dying and the dead are for living."[15] But it is all Life. And Life is eternal. It spirals on in one way or another. Stumped by the elusive mysteries of its transitional phases, we apply labels to them: Birth, Life, Death. "The body," wrote the sixteenth-century Rabbi Yeshayahu ben Avraham, "**lives** in a momentary occurrence, and then

---

[12] First Samuel 28:6-15
[13] Ecclesiastes 3:2
[14] *Midrash Tanchuma, Pikudei*, Ch. 3
[15] *Mishnah, Avot* 4:22

is essentially **dead**; the soul, on the other hand, **dies** in a momentary occurrence, and then is essentially **alive**."[16]

This understanding of death as being far from any ending, any definitive culmination, gave rise to numerous rituals surrounding the course of dying and of death itself. Respect for the dead, honoring the dead, praying at the sites of tombs and graves, all became an integral part of Judaic consciousness and practice. If death is not the end, then we continue to be in relationship with those who came before us and with those who have passed on in our life time, particularly with close of kin and other loved ones, as well as with teachers and other persons who have played positive roles in the unfolding of our lives. When we quote the teachings of a master, the ancient rabbis taught, "their lips move in the grave along with the words we are quoting."[17]

While we continue our relationship with those who have passed on, whether by interaction in one form or another, or by mere memory, we thereby also retain our connection with the realm beyond the realm we know. In this way, what we call "death" becomes less a stranger to us, and more a shift from one reality to another, from one universe to another. Our sense of there being more to life than life itself is vital to our being able to muster forth meaningfulness and purpose to our being, and to our endeavors at self-growth and personal ennoblement.

Facing our death is akin to preparing our bed, so to speak, readying our deepest core selves for the unknown next. Therefore, it has for millennia been Jewish practice to prepare for sleep as if we were preparing for death. The night time ritual actually includes prayers that one would say upon dying, since sleep is considered "one-sixtieth of death."[18] Even in our waking moments, each step we dare take into our next instant is in itself a death, a small one, but a death nonetheless. No less than death, every next moment is an unknown, an arena of uncertainty, a complete mystery waiting to be encountered and engaged, a passageway to a whole other universe of possibility, and totally unpredictable. Yet,

---

[16] *Sefer HaSh'lah, Torah Ohr, Bamidbar-Devarim, Parashat Pinchas*, No. 1
[17] *Talmud Yerushalmi, Shekalim* 11a
[18] *Talmud Bav'li, B'rachot* 57b

we meet it head-on day to day, hour to hour, minute to minute, dying and rebirthing, dying and rebirthing, not only existentially but also biologically as the very cells of our bodies are continually dying and renewing. It is here, then, in the drama of this lifetime, that we make our preparations, that we ready ourselves, that we fix what needs fixing, straighten what needs straightening, and clear what needs clearing, so that our evolution, our journey across the chasm of this ever-mysterious existence, might continue unabated. "This world," taught the third-century Rabbi Yanai, "is likened onto a lobby in relation to the World that is Coming. Prepare yourself in the lobby, so that you might enter the main hall."[19]

Death is then very sacred, to be revered not out of fear or dread but out of respect for its vivid reminder to us of the deeper meaning of **Life**, that life is a thread weaving itself through many realms, not only the ones we are aware of; that there is more to life than it's cracked up to be. "The mystery of an afterlife," wrote Abraham Joshua Heschel, "is related to the mystery of preexistence. A soul does not grow out of nothing. Does it, then, perish and **dissolve** into nothing?"[20]

The sanctity and importance of death is best dramatized in the story of the ancestral father of the Jewish people, Abraham, a narrative that includes a very extensive dialogue and negotiation with a clan of Hittites over a piece of land he had chosen for burying his wife Sarah, the ancestral **mother** of the Jews. That he paid a heap of money and went through extensive negotiations to acquire a particular piece of property for her burial, and that the Torah spends an entire chapter detailing those negotiations and the final acquisition of this small piece of acreage,[21] demonstrates how dear the dead are to us; how our endearment toward the living does not die with them; how we do not relate to the dead in the land of the living with glib dismissal. Abraham went through so much effort in negotiating for the burial site he chose for Sarah in order to impart to us this very lesson, that death is sacred,

---

[19] *Mishnah, Avot* 4:16
[20] *Reflections on Death* [Farrar, Straus, and Giraux, Inc.]
[21] Genesis, Chapter 23

and that the soul lives on, thus the need to honor the physical vehicles of departed souls with decent burial, not arbitrary disposal.

Accordingly, the Hebrew ancestress Sarah's death is heralded in terms of her life, that she lived a qualitative life, and therefore her death, too, was precious,[22] "for the righteous ones, even in their deaths are called 'Living.'"[23] Those who behave wickedly toward others and perpetuate harm and destruction, are considered as dead, to begin with[24] – that is, of never having **lived**, "for the soul is in death as she is in life."[25] This is borne-out in the Book of Ezekiel where God says: "For I do not desire the death of the already-dead. But that they return [repent] and **live**."[26]

There were many who lived beautiful, mindful lives, and were tragically martyred, sometimes through drawn-out trauma and torture, yet their death – as tragic as it was – retained the same quality as their life. They neither lost their faith nor surrendered their beliefs and convictions. They died as they lived.

Some 2,300 years ago, Alexander the Great asked the Hebrew sages of the Negev: "If one wishes to die, what should one do?" They replied: "One should **live**."[27] Meaning, the quality we invest in living later translates into the quality we reap in dying. Or as the second-century Rabbi Sh'mu'el admonished his colleague Rabbi Yehudah: "Seize and eat! Seize and drink! For the world that we are leaving behind is like a wedding reception!"[28] – in other words, try to enjoy life while you're here. The more we celebrate living, the better prepared we will be for the transition into dying, because the empowerment gained from the celebration of life will carry us through the evolution of death. "The

---

[22] Genesis 23:1; *Midrash Bereisheet Rabbah* 58:1
[23] *Talmud Bav'li, Berachot* 18a
[24] *Midrash Kohelet Rabbah* 9:4
[25] *Sefer Chassidim*, No. 1129
[26] Ezekiel 18:32
[27] *Talmud Bav'li, Tamid* 32a
[28] *Talmud Bavli, Eruvin* 54a

fact of dying," wrote Rabbi Abraham Joshua Heschel, "must be a major factor in our understanding of living."[29]

When the 18th-century Rabbi Simcha Bunim of Pzsyczka was about to depart from this world, his wife stood by his bedside and broke out in tears. He looked up at her, puzzled, and asked: "Why do you cry? Do you not realize that the purpose of my entire life was so that I might know how to die?"[30]

The lesson inherent in investing the amount of energy, time and expenditures in tending to those no longer with us is a lesson in altruism, a practice that in itself does not benefit the dead nearly as much as it benefits the living, deepening our sensitivity and conscientiousness. Tending to the dead is therefore considered in Judaism as among the highest deeds of lovingkindness one could possibly perform since there is no gratitude or recompense forthcoming from the deceased.[31] It is indeed a training of the human spirit toward altruistic thought and action, promoting personal and communal moral ennoblement and deepening of consciousness. Since tending to the dead is an act of benevolence for which there is nothing in return, it is called *Chessed shel Emet* חסד של אמת, literally: "Lovingkindness of [a] **True** [nature]."[32] This is implied in the Torah's account of the death of the ancestor Jacob, who declared to his children that the fulfillment of his dying wish would be "an act of lovingkindness and of truth."[33]

While the Torah makes no mention of what happens after death, other than we join our ancestors,[34] Judaism's equally rich **oral** tradition does offer more specific teachings, that when we die we are greeted by the first human couple, Adam and Eve,[35] and by people we knew in our

---

[29] *Moral Grandeur and Spiritual Audacity* (Noonday Press), p.366

[30] *Histalkut HaNefesh*

[31] 11th-century Rabbi Shlomo Yitzchaki [Rashi] on Genesis 47:29; see also 16th-century Rabbi Yeshayahu ben Avraham in *Sefer HaShLaH, Mesechet Pesachim, Perek Ner Mitzvah*, No. 50

[32] *Midrash Bereisheet Rabbah* 96:5

[33] Genesis 47:29

[34] e.g., Genesis 25:8 and 49:29 and 33

[35] *Sefer Ha'Sh'LaH, Chayyai Sarah, Torah Ohr*, No. 1

lifetime who had passed on earlier.³⁶ Loving relatives and friends who have passed before us join-in on the reception and help guide us gently through the process of our transition.³⁷ There is no lack of wisdom in this ancient tradition around life after death. Yet, the emphasis of the teachers has always been on Life, on living in the here-and-now. And while they taught about the eventual resurrection of the dead,³⁸ not all the sages held this belief as a mandatory principle of the Jewish faith.³⁹ They taught about עולם הבא *O'lam Ha'Ba*, or the "World that is Coming," and how the soul lives on after death – yes – but they encouraged a greater focus on Life in the Land of the Living. "I want to walk before God," wrote the Hebrew tribal chieftain David some 3,000 years ago, "and witness the good of God in the land of the **living**."⁴⁰ The Torah herself is referred to as a tree of **Life**, חיים עץ*Etz Chayyim*.⁴¹

Judaism's emphasis on the preciousness of the here-and-now is so central that it moved the third-century Rabbi Ya'akov to declare: "More precious is a single moment of personal transformation and the performance of positive deeds in **this** world than an eternity in the World that is Coming!"⁴² Not to downplay the promised bliss of the next world, Rabbi Ya'akov then added: "And more precious is a single moment of **bliss** in the World that is Coming than an entire lifetime [of bliss] in **this** world." The difference is clear. "Death," wrote Abraham Joshua Heschel, "is not understood as the end of **being**, but rather as the end of **doing**."⁴³ Life is 9-to-5. Death is an eternal vacation, paid-in-full by our struggles and how we dealt with them; by our challenges and how we overcame them. And sometimes, those struggles and challenges are so intense that we would in those moments gladly give up any amount of accrued vacation time in the World-that-is-yet-to-Come for

---

³⁶ *Ma'avar Ya'vok*, Ch. 32
³⁷ *Zohar*, Vol. 1, folio 218b
³⁸ *Mishnah, Sotah* 9:15, *Sanhedrin* 10:1
³⁹ e.g. Yosef Albo in *Sefer Ha'Ikkarim* Vol. 1, Chapter 29, No. 31
⁴⁰ Psalms 27:13 and 116:9
⁴¹ Proverbs 3:18
⁴² *Mishna, Avot* 4:17
⁴³ *Reflections on Death* [Farrar, Straus, and Giraux, Inc.], p. 71)

some respite from our sufferings in the here-and-now. As one suffering rabbi put it some 1,900 years ago: "I prefer neither the suffering nor its reward."[44]

Death is then an integral part of Being. As the 3rd-century **B.C.E.** sage Ben-Sira taught: "Do not fear death. Remember, there were people that have been here before you, and there will be people here **after** you. This is God's scheme of things for all of us, so why are you so against **this** particular piece of the Divine Plan?"[45] And as the Wise Woman of Te'ko'ah told King David some 700 years earlier: "We must all die; we are like water spilt upon the earth, which cannot be gathered up again."[46] In other words, once we are created, we are like water trickling into the earth never again to manifest as what was, but to emerge anew as what is yet to be; we seep deeper and deeper into Being-ness; we **are**, forever. Therefore, while we are taught the importance of grieving over the dead, we are also discouraged against **excessive** grieving. The Talmud put it this way: "One who grieves to excess over a death may end up creating a situation in which they will be grieving over another death."[47] Yet, to exercise self-control and force oneself **not** to grieve when the anguish is flowing; to not allow oneself to feel what is, is foolish. The rules are there as general guidelines built upon the laws of averages; they are not intended as do-or-die mandates: "And you shall **live** by these teachings"[48] – to which the ancient rabbis add: "And not kill yourself over them."[49] A precedential example is the biblical story of the Hebrew patriarch Jacob, who refused all attempts at consolation and expressed a degree of grief over the presumed death of his son Joseph that was so intense that he vowed to take it with him to the grave![50]

---

[44] *Talmud Bav'li, Berachot* 5b
[45] Ecclestiasticus 41:3-4
[46] Second Samuel 14:14
[47] *Talmud Bavli, Mo'ed Katan* 27b
[48] Leviticus 18:6 and Ezekiel 20:11
[49] *Midrash Kohelet Rabbah* 1:24
[50] Genesis 37:35

What happens when we die? We cannot know. Like Moses told us more than 3,300 years ago: "The hidden things are for *yhwh* our God; the revealed things are for us and for our children."[51]

> And the Wisdom -- where will you find it? And in what place is Understanding? Humanity does not know its depth, and you will not find it in the Land of the Living. The Abyss declares, "She is not within me"; and the Sea declares, "Nor with me." And the Wisdom -- from where does she come? And in what place is Understanding? And she vanishes from the eyes of all beings, and is hidden from the birds of the skies. Loss and Death declare: "In our ears we have heard a pronouncement: 'Only *Elo'heem* understands her path, and knows the place where she is.'"[52]

What we **do** know from our ancestors, however, is that we return to where we came from, to God who made us. That even when our bodies give-in, our souls live on. "Whom have I in the Heavens," wrote King David, "but you, O God. And I desire nothing here on Earth but you. Though my flesh and my heart fail, God is my rock and my thread of continuity forever."[53] Here, too, we see how Judaism, from ancient times, held life as a continuous journey from beyond to here and then back to beyond. What happens to our soul after we die is called *hash'arat nefesh*, meaning: "the continuation of the soul," that although the body is gone from life, the soul **remains** in Life. We see this belief reflected in the words of an ancient Hebrew wise-woman named Abigail (c. 1,000 B.C.E.) who blessed King David with the following: "May you be bound-up in the bundle of Life in the care of *YHWH* your God."[54]

And since departed souls remain in the bigger picture of what we glibly refer to as Life, they, too, are as curious about the living as the living are about the dead. At times, therefore, they roam around the world to see what's happening here, and what fate looms ahead for us

---

[51] Deuteronomy 29:28
[52] Job 28:20-23
[53] Psalms 73:25-26
[54] First Samuel 25:29

living folk.[55] At times, they even visit us for the purpose of guiding us, and well-meaningly might even suggest that we follow them. But this can cause us to die, we are warned. So if that ever happens to you, bare your feet so that you are in real-time connection with the earth, with life in **this** realm, and repeat three times: "I want to be in this life, in this world. Do not return ever again, neither to me, neither to my children."[56] This disclaimer, or warning, sits right for most of us, as the average person is unprepared for dealing wholesomely with a visitation from someone who has crossed over. Of course, there are exceptions, namely in regards to those individuals who are capable of remaining centered if such visitations were to occur, and who would not react with terror and possibly experience cardiac arrest.

In the course of their roaming ventures, the dead are able to return to the land of the living when they wish, and can appear to us in any form they desire.[57] They may at times communicate with us, but only when they want to. However, they do not appreciate being conjured,[58] and when they **do** visit us they will usually visit us while we are in a dream state, and sometimes even while we are awake.[59] However, the dead are not allowed to reveal to us secrets of the heavens,[60] and if they come to us in our dreams and offer us an item, there are two schools of thought about whether we should receive it from them: the Talmud says No; the Zohar says Yes, and that it is in fact a good omen.[61] It would make sense that the dead would at times communicate with us in our dreams since the dream state itself is believed to be one-sixtieth of the death state.[62] Still, it is important to consult a learned teacher regarding these matters since any such endeavors require strong presence of mind and body, and groundedness, and is not for everyone to dabble

---

[55] *Talmud Bavli, B'rachot* 18b
[56] Will and Testament of 12th-century Rabbi Yehudah Ha'Chassid, No. 9
[57] *Sefer Chassidim*, No. 1129
[58] First Samuel 28:13
[59] *Sefer Chassidim*, No. 1128
[60] *Sefer Chassidim*, No. 1133
[61] Zohar, Vol. 4, folio 180a
[62] *Talmud Bavli, B'rachot* 57b

in. When the portals of the other realms open to us, we must be rock-solid certain before we engage in any part of welcoming what is coming through by participating in the process of opening that gate. Those on the other side can open the door, but only from **their** side; they cannot enter without the cooperation of we who walk in the Land of the Living, without us opening the door on **our** end as well. To do so requires years of deep mystical studies and practice, and is not for most of us. Like the old TV adage goes: "Do not try this at home."

The ancients also considered the experience of sexual orgasm as a taste of the afterlife. It is probably the closest glimpse we can have of the realm beyond this life. Why *sex*, as opposed to, say, a mouth-watering pizza? Ordinarily the body experiences blissfulness from what it takes **in**, whether food or sensuous touch. But in sex, the body experiences bliss by what it sends **out**, by what it surrenders of itself – which is what happens at death, when the body sends out the soul, releases its final breath, surrendering of its Self. Thus, the sages taught that sexual climaxing is akin to the bliss waiting for us in the afterlife.[63] Death is a lesson in surrender, surrender to our faith in the unknowable, our trust in the process and in the mystery that moves **it** through us and we through **it**.

> What happens to the Human and what happens to the Animal, it is all one happening. As the death for this one, so is the death for the other; and one breath do they all share. And the advantage of the Human over the Animal is nil, for it is all vanity. In the end, all go to one place; for all originated from the soil and it is to the soil that all return. Who knows the spirit of the Human, whether she ascends above [to the heavens]; and the spirit of the Animal, whether she descends below onto the earth? And I have seen that there is nothing better than a person rejoicing in their accomplishments, for that is what they have been allotted. For who will ever bring us to see what it is that comes after all this?[64]

---

[63] *Talmud Bavli, B'rachot* 57b
[64] Ecclesiastes 3:19-22

CHAPTER TWO

The Invitation

> "**And behold! It was *very* good!**"[65] – this refers to **Death**.[66]

Very good? **Death?**

Indeed. Can you imagine what it would be like if all that was is all that is? The phenomenon of Death, the ancients taught, assures us that our existence involves far more than what we experience in the here-and-now as Life. "***Very*** Good" moves us beyond the mediocrity of merely that which is okay as is and directs us toward horizons of possibility that traverse "the way it is" to the mystery of "what is yet to be," which, as the ancient Hebrew prophet Isaiah put it: "No eye has seen it, except yours, O Master of All Powers and of all Capabilities."[67]

"And it was Good" – this is the definition of what we have, of what is in front of us. "And it was **Very** Good" – this is the indefinable mystery of Next and Other, of all that is so totally different from anything we can know while we are here. It is Death. After all, Death is the elusive, unknowable Next, and the awesome, mysterious Other, as in a reality other than the only reality we know while we meander about in what we refer to as Life.

Death is the snake shedding its skin, the soul shedding its embodiment, the fetus shedding its placenta. In other words, rather

---

[65] Genesis 1:31
[66] Zohar, Vol. 1, folio 47a
[67] Isaiah 64:3

than the end of Life, it is a Rebirth, a **continuation** of Living. Thus did Solomon write that there is "a season for Birthing and a season for Dying."[68] As mentioned earlier, he deliberately worded it this way, rather than "a season for **Living** and a season for Dying," to remind us that living is always, whereas birthing and dying are but intermittent phases within the drama behind the mystery of Living, the drama of being which we experience along the infinite pathways of Living. Death is but yet another Birth into yet another Life. It is not a state of being but a state of transitioning. We were originally born in the primordial *Thought* of God, out of which we then died and were birthed into the individuated *Spirit* Realm, out of which we died and were born into the physical *Womb* Realm, out of which we died and were born into **this** lifetime, out of which we will one day die and be born into that which "no eye has seen but yours, O God." We can therefore only speak of Death in terms of Life.

"And God saw that it was טוב *to'v* -- Good," means that this is as it ought to be. In other words: What you see is what you get. Period. This is all there is. This and nothing more. "**Very** Good," on the other hand, extends that seeming boundary of the known, of the defined, beyond its established finite nature into the infinite expanses of endless possibility. Death is then the flinging open of the portals of boundary and limitation out to the infinite, untold realms of alternative forms of being and becoming. And Life is the continuous journey of transition and evolution, the journey that threads us from one portal to the next, from Birthing to Dying to Birthing.

Evidence of this ongoing voyage is the undisputable fact that the moment we are born, we are already on our way toward dying. The act of **living**, in other words, is actually the act of **dying**! There is nothing on the horizon that follows Birth, other than Death. We are in essence always on our way out, ascending and descending on a single ladder embedded in the earth while simultaneously reaching for the heavens

---

[68] Ecclesiastes 3:2

beyond,[69] inhaling and exhaling at the same time, birthing and dying in the same moment, a moment defined as "Living."

It is by our working with what we **do** know and encounter in the here-and-now, however, that we ready ourselves by default for what is yet to come, that we seed our relationship with death while we are yet alive. This is a challenging spiritual practice for most of us, as it involves working at letting go of the very objective we seek to engage. The pathway to a good death, in other words, is a good life, a positive, conscientious participation in the gift of the moment, for every moment is an episode of death and rebirth, dying out of what was and birthing into what is. If we live every moment strictly on the basis of the moment that **was**, we end up missing out on what could have been.

Legend has it that when the first-century Caesar Augustus was traveling through Judea, he noticed an elderly man busily planting a fig tree. He halted his horse and asked the elder his age. "I am 100 years old," the man replied. "Well, then why do you bother planting?" laughed Caesar. After all, the old man would never live long enough to see his sapling grow and bear fruit! So why bother? The elder replied that if he didn't live another couple of years to see it bear fruit, at least his children and grandchildren would.[70]

This story is about focusing-in on the gift of the moment without being distracted by the possible down-side of our assumptions of the future, or the "result." We see this in an earlier teaching, in the ancient writ of the Hebrew prophet Jeremiah, where, in his prophecy around the Babylonian exile of the Jews, he quotes God as saying: "Thus says God to the entire community, 'I have exiled you from Jerusalem to Babylon. Nonetheless, build homes there, and settle in them, and plant gardens, and continue perpetuating families, children...and seek the peace of the villages to which I have exiled you....'"[71]

In other words, even though the future looked bleak -- exile, the destruction of the Jewish commonwealth, subjection to another

---

[69] Genesis 28:12

[70] *Midrash Tanchuma, Kedoshim*, Ch. 8

[71] Jeremiah 29:4-7

culture, etc. – the Hebrew ancestors were implored to not allow the seeming forecast to dampen the gift of their moment, and were instead encouraged to make the best of the moment, build homes in the exile, marry, start families, plant gardens, orchards, not get caught up in what **was** or in what might have **been**, but in what **is**; to seek out the gift of the moment and then seize it and make the best of it. It is this difficult but important mindset that enabled the Jewish nation to survive and flourish through what was to become the longest and most tragic exile ever to befall any one group. According to this mindset, we are in constant flux of birthing and dying, the act of living being the thread that weaves through both dramas, binding the two into a singular existential fabric we call "Moment."

A moment, then, is more than a marker of time; it is an infinite galaxy of possibilities, each possibility having been created before time itself in the cauldron of Genesis, waiting forever for its turn, for its time to be invited, to be conjured, to be called into existence, and only at **that** very moment. No other moment would do, because every moment is a distinct portal through which any given aspect of infinite Creation and possibility might emerge and manifest. In every single moment, therefore, your persona shifts; you are freed from who you were until that moment. You look the same and feel no inherent difference, but know that you are not the same. You are rather free to transform, to become someone different, and to choose a whole different way of relating to your partner, your children, your employees, your boss, your Self. Every moment is an opportunity to enrich your life by embracing your death, by letting go of what was, in order to create space for what can be.

The word in Hebrew for "Moment" is זמן *z'mahn*. Interestingly, *z'mahn* is also the Hebraic word for "Invitation." Every moment is an invitation, an invitation to step out of where you have been and into where you are now invited. Not coincidentally, the Hebraic word traditionally employed to describe the act of dying is נפטר *nif'tar*, which literally translates as "released," or "exempt." The moment, in other words, is an invitation to enter and to leave, to birth and to die, to basically be **released** from that illusion which binds you to the finite and fossilizes you in the familiar to the neglect of the possible.

A moment is either in constant flux of renewal, or stagnant on its way to burn-out. It all depends on whether we **engage** the moment or simply let it run by us. Time moves you whether you are on board or not, whether you are in sync with it and aware of it, or not. And you, in turn, take the lead in your ongoing dance with Time during those moments when you become aware of and consciously interact with Time. When you step out of the humdrum of the moment to **participate** in the moment, you then meet your dance partner eye-to-eye and the encounter becomes in that moment intimate. This is the הזמנה *haz'manah* of the זמן *z'mahn*, "the invitation of the moment." When you accept the invitation of the moment, you make it sacred, you give it meaning by conscious intention and in that way release the moment from its constriction within Finite Time and send it beyond Finite Time into the Realm of Infinity, beyond the transitory nature of that which is. Conscious intention -- or in Hebrew: כונה *kavanah* -- filters the moment, removing from within it the impediments of limitations and hopelessness so that it might be released into the infinite horizon of possibility. This quality of intention asks you to be in the moment, to take hold of the thread of Divine Consciousness that lives within you and weave it into whatever is happening in that moment. You thereby invite God to see through your eyes, to partner with you in your life walk. The mortal thus invites the immortal into the moment by sacred intention, and thereby creates a God Space by which he or she also open up the chutes of Divine Presence and Divine Flux – or *shefa* שפע in Hebrew -- to be more vividly immanent. That event is then touched by the Divine which renders that moment infinite.

So when you acknowledge the gift of what you are about to experience, conscious of its origination in the intent of the Great Mystery out of which all emanates, then, in that very moment, you attach your intention to the One whose intention enables the very existence of, say, food, or sex, or…moment. You connect your intention around the temporary existence of that particular pleasure of which you are about to partake, to the One who made it possible, and who in itself is infinite. Resultantly, that very delicious moment or encounter or experience will always remain with you, for you have in that moment **freed** the encounter from its finite realm, from its "Good," to its infinite realm, to its "**Very** Good," by infusing it with the infinite nature of the very gesture that brought it to you in the moment. You have in essence accepted "the invitation of the moment."

The fourteenth-century mystic Rabbi Bach'ya ibn Yosef Paquda offered the parable of the sailor whose shipwrecked body washed-up ashore on a strange and distant island. When he regained consciousness he was shocked to find himself surrounded by hordes of native islanders, all of whom were prostrating to him as if he were some kind of demigod. Others were busily removing his shredded garments and replacing them with a diamond-studded leopard skin robe, and before he could catch his breath he was lifted up high upon a portable throne and carried through the village for all to behold and honor. The natives next brought him to a beautiful palace laden with riches beyond his imagination and, to make a long story short, he ended up with a wife of great beauty and had many children and lived happily ever after.

That is, until one day it began to bother him. Like, what's the catch? And so he summoned one of his trusted servants and asked pointedly: "What's the catch?" To which the servant replied: "Well, since you have asked, I must answer. You see, there have been many before you, strangers from afar who have been shipwrecked and ended up on our shores. It has long been our tradition to take them in and make them king or queen of our island for a period of ten years, after which we then escort them back to the beach, remove their royal garb, return to them their shrouds and send them off to sea on a simple raft in the direction of whence they came."

When the king heard this, he panicked! "But I love my wife, my children, and all of my riches. I can't just leave it all behind!!"

"Your Majesty," said the servant, "there is a solution. If I were you, I would invest time and energy right now to send it all home while you still have it!"

And so, that is exactly what the king did. He shipped everything and everyone he loved back to the country of his origin, so that when his tenure was up and they escorted him to the raft waiting for him on the seashore, he indeed did leave with nothing at all, but was heading back to where all was waiting for him to enjoy uninterruptedly for the rest of his life.[72]

The moral of the story is that you **can** take it with you. Dying is not about **leaving** Life; it's about **living** Life. It's about making your every moment count, making your time here-and-now **mean** something, not only to others but to yourself as well. Living involves the art of noticing, of being present enough to recognize and identify the invitation of the moment. And by "invitation" is meant the act of joining the everyday, the so-called mundane, with the sacred; bonding the finite with the infinite. In the words of Abraham Joshua Heschel: "It is not in our power to transport the beyond to become here; but we can transport the here to the beyond."[73]

In the Hebrew scriptural story of what is popularly known as "The Ten Commandments," the people experience the earth-shattering revelatory drama of God speaking directly to them following their liberation from centuries of bondage in Egypt. The direct encounter with the Creator proves to be far too mind-blowing for them, and so they plead with Moses to intercept the Divine Revelation and deliver the remaining message himself in mortal terms.[74] Moses then ascends the mountain and spends well over a month inside a dark cloud where he is given the remainder of the intended instructions to the people. Days go by, weeks go by, and some of the people grow restless, wondering what has become of Moses their leader, their one and only intermediary between them and God, their one and only guide across the Sinai Desert toward their ancestral homeland. In panic, they turn to Moses' elder brother Aaron who, in an attempt to stall the rabble, gathers from them their jewelry, melts it into a nice hefty chunk of gold, and throws it into a bonfire out of which emerges a golden calf.[75] The people immediately treat the edifice as a Moses-substitute and some

---

[72] *Cho'vo't Hal'va'vo't, Sha'ar Avodat Elo'heem*, Ch. 9
[73] *Man is not Alone*, p. 131
[74] Exodus 20:16
[75] Exodus 32:1-6

of them even begin to worship it as a demigod, infusing the sculpture with their illusion of a symbolic representation of the divine force that redeemed them from bondage. They panicked because "Moses delayed in descending from the mountain." They panicked because, how they had locked themselves into defining the moment was not adding up. They were fixated more on what the moment **ought** to look like rather than remain open to "the invitation of the moment."

Among the many lessons of this story is this: You need to wait patiently for the invitation and to be aware of the fact that your whole process of being, of living, of unfolding, is not made or broken by whether the moment invites you or not. For example: Let's say you just found out that your best friend is getting married. Upon hearing this exciting news, you begin to anxiously anticipate getting an invitation in the mail. Days go by, weeks go by; you grow increasingly anxious and wonder what has happened to your anticipated invitation. Eventually, your desperation drives you to hire a graphic artist and to create your own invitation to your friend's wedding which you then print and mail to yourself. The fixation has now transitioned from the excitement around your friend's pending marriage to your urgency around being invited, so that in the end you are left with a bogus substitutive illusion that heralds neither the joy of celebrating your friend's marriage nor the elimination of your anxiety around being invited. You have succeeded in conjuring an invitation, but one that is replete with misguidance regarding time and place, let alone date and program.

An old Jewish parable:

Once there was a dog who heard that there were two weddings going on, one nearby and one a couple miles away. Salivating at the thought of leftover meat-strewn bones and discarded fat, the dog decided to beeline it first to the distant reception and then later he would head for the one nearby. His logic was simple and sensible: If he were to first gorge himself at the nearby party, by the time he would finish gnawing and head all the way out to the distant one, the distant wedding reception would be all done and there would be no leftovers remaining. So best to go first to the distant one, he thought.

Extremely proud of his decision, the dog hurried to the far-away wedding reception -- but alas, it turned out to be farther than he thought so that by the time he finally got there, the party was over, and everything had been cleaned up. Hungry, he dashed all the way back to the original reception -- but alas, by the time he arrived, it was all over and done and not a scrap remained. Bottom line, he benefited from neither the one nor the other and ended up with nothing.[76]

In hindsight, of course, had the dog simply focused on the invitation of the moment, and settled for the first of the wedding receptions rather than go for both, he would have had a feast -- perhaps not everything that he'd envisioned, but certainly a mouthful. Like the ancient rabbis put it: "Seize a lot and you come away with nothing; seize but a little, and you will at least have something."[77]

This is the challenge of your life journey. Can you see every moment as an invitation for you to step daringly out of the rote flow of your unconscious impulse, or will you freeze Time to examine the invitation? We cannot judge the value of an invitation until we get there.

In the Ten Commandments story, the people had gathered around the mountain waiting for a particular moment to invite them, an invitation from Moses, master of the Exodus, facilitator of Divine Revelation. This exclusive focus on the man Moses diverted their focus from other precious moments that came and went, precious moments of looking into the eyes of a lover, of showing affection to one's children, of extending a helping hand to a neighbor, and so on. The subsequent vacuum that they thereby created happened to manifest as a Golden Calf, but it wouldn't have mattered if it would have turned out to be a Golden Hamster or a Golden Chicken, as long as it was **something** – anything —which intent was to aid them in regaining some semblance of focus. And regain their focus they did, and they rejoiced and celebrated and partied. They now had their Moses-substitute, their surrogate reference point. Modern psychology calls this "transference." And that was okay,

---

[76] *Sefer Ben Melech V'Ha'Nazir*
[77] *Talmud Bav'li, Yoma* 80a

until the people sacrificed to it and worshiped it, so that what started out as innocent transference soon turned into misplaced intimacy.

It is not insignificant that, according to traditional Judaic teaching, none of the Israelite women were involved in the Golden Calf fiasco. Many women are by their very nature more attuned to Time, to Moment, to the Invitation. They are the carriers of both Life and Death. It is by the death of a soul in the spirit world that it is reborn into the womb world of woman, and it is by the death of a soul in the womb world that it is reborn into this world, again, by way of woman. This is why, in Jewish religious law, women are exempt from all ritual requirements that are time-bound, time oriented.[78] The feminine is naturally in touch with the sanctity of Moment, and there is therefore no requirement for a Jewish woman to pray at particular times of the day as is required of Jewish men, and in ancient times, although women participated *en-masse* in all three of the seasonal pilgrimages to the Temple Mount in Jerusalem, they were not obligated to do so, whereas the men were.[79] Women tend to live-out through their bodies and emotions the drama of Spring, Summer and Autumn, by way of puberty, conception, and menopause.

Since most women, by their very nature, were more in cadence with the rhythm and sanctity of Moment, they were more capable of dealing with Moses' delay in descending from the mountain. They did not experience the delay as a vacuum in time but as the very build-up toward the crescendo that would, at the **right** time, reveal itself as the invitation of the moment. The ancient rabbis further taught that following the incident of the Golden Calf, the role of Keepers of the Renewal of Moon was removed from the men and assigned to the women[80] since they were better attuned to being in a more sacred relationship with the phases of Moon, the phases of waxing and waning, of birthing, dying, and rebirth.[81] The men waited those 40 days and 40 nights fixated on one anticipated moment, waiting for one particular, pre-defined moment,

---

[78] *Talmud Bav'li, Berachot* 20b
[79] Exodus 23:17, 34:23, and Deuteronomy 16:16
[80] *Midrash Pir'kei D'Rebbe Eliezer*, Ch. 45
[81] see Rabbi Miriam Maron's book, *Ancient Moon Wisdom* [Hamilton Books, 2013]

while many other precious moments whizzed right by them, creating thereby a serious vacuum which they then attempted to fill with the Golden Calf, an illusory representation of their self-created moment, their self-created invitation. In other words, they reached desperately for a moment whose invitation had not yet arrived.

A similar example is that of the much earlier Hebraic story of the first human couple, the proverbial Adam and Eve, and the first proverbial human mistake: plucking the proverbial forbidden fruit from the proverbial tree of knowledge of good and not-so-good. The question in the minds of the ancient teachers of this tradition centered around the puzzling act of God planting a fruit tree in the Garden of Eden that was off limits. If the intent was for it not to be eaten from, then why plant it, to begin with? Is fruit not *intended* to be plucked from the tree? How else are we supposed to eat it? And the answer is that the fruit, although intended for your consumption and pleasure, is never to be *severed* from the tree. Rather, you must wait for the tree to *release* it; you must wait until it has ripened, at which time the tree will release it to you; you must wait for the season of its ripening; you must wait for the invitation of the moment. The snake in this story -- the Jewish version of what in some aboriginal traditions might be considered the "Trickster" -- does not lie. Rather, the Trickster has you so intrigued by the appearance of the fruit, yet unripe, that, for all intents and purposes, it *appears* ready for the picking when it isn't.

When the Serpent told Eve that she couldn't eat of the tree because God knows she will become filled with the wisdom of God, he was telling the truth, but out of context. The truth was, indeed the Tree of Knowledge would gift them with more Divine Wisdom than they could ever dream possible, specifically the simultaneous awareness of Good and Evil – not one *or* the other, or one *and* the other, but both at the same time in the same moment. In truth, that capacity of knowing would be theirs the moment they bit into the fruit, and even God Itself later admits as much.[82] But what the Serpent did **not** tell them

---

[82] Genesis 3:22

was that **timing** was of the essence, that the fruit needed to ripen first before any of this would become possible. Indeed, the ancient teachers insisted, had Adam and Eve waited one more day, they would have been permitted to eat it,[83] for it would have become fully ripened by then. So when they **did** eat of the fruit, their eyes "opened" and the stream of Divine Wisdom began to flow toward them, albeit un-ripened and thus deficient. The ink on the pending invitation had barely dried, and so the premature plucking of the fruit, of the invitation, yielded a communication that had become smudged, its intended information distorted and illegible. Consequently, this ancient story informs us, the human struggle is very much about surmounting the blurred nature of the line between Good and Evil. And accompanying this struggle is the human discomfort with the blurred nature of the line between Life and Death as well.

The art of recognizing and identifying the invitation of the moment requires us to understand Moment as an instantaneous death and rebirth. This is why suicide is antithetical to waiting for the invitation of Death, the invitation to be reborn into the next reality. It is akin to writing your own invitation to an event that hasn't been planned, let alone arranged. It is the act of plucking the fruit in its yet un-ripened state rather than waiting for the tree to release it as the juicy, wholesome gift it was intended. Resurrection is not confined to some religious hope of future, pending the "end of times." It is what is occurring right now as you read these words. You have died and resurrected, died and rebirthed a hundred thousand times over the span of time it took for you to read this sentence. Even modern science realizes this truth, informing us that in every moment our physical bodies are dying and rebirthing, that the cells which comprise our bodily infrastructure are continuously and simultaneously dying and regenerating. The natural phenomenon of cellular dying, which is a healthy and necessary process in human growth and development, is known as "apoptosis," programmed cell death, and is a result of what we might consider the cell's harmonious

---

[83] 18th-century Rabbi Moshe Sofer, quoted in Rabbi Efraim Zeitchik's *Torat HaNefesh*, folio 48

interplay and acceptance of the invitation of the moment. On the other hand, the radical, uncontrollable phenomenon of cellular birthing at an unusual rate, which is unhealthy to human growth and development, is known as "cancer," and is the result of what we might consider the cell's ***forcing*** an invitation to a moment that isn't ripe.

This is the deeper, underlying meaning of an otherwise puzzling verse in the ancient Song of Solomon -- or, in Hebrew, *Shir Ha'Shirim* שיר השירים, literally: Song of [all] the Songs -- regarded by the second-century Rabbi Akiva as the most sacred of all the Hebrew Scriptures, literally "The Holy of Holies."[84] The verse reads as follows: "I made you swear an oath, O Daughters of Jerusalem, that you not awaken the love until your desire [has awakened]."[85] On a simplistic level, the wisdom of Solomon here implores us not to **force** intimacy, but to rather wait for the arousal of mutual desire before attempting intimate interaction. A love awakened before it is ripe is a repeat of the Garden of Eden fiasco as well as that of the Golden Calf. On a deeper level, Solomon is alluding to the human tendency – and that of the institution of Religion in particular – to not only continually promise but continually vie for the end of times before its time; to promise and endeavor toward bringing about the proverbial Utopian dream before its time, the prophetic ideal behind this being far short of anything over which we wield any control, for "no eye has beheld it, O Elo'heem, but yours."[86] Whether we label the Utopian ideal Messianic or Hereafter or World-that-is-Coming, Solomon has God entreating humankind to vow not to pluck the fruit before it is ripened, not to **force** the hoped-for era of the ultimate Divine Promise of the unknown Next.

The hope of that vision, in all of its versions, is that we would one day experience soul and body in a reality absent the responsibilities, struggles, tragedies and suffering with which we now grapple. In the here-and-now, we only have a glimpse of that kind of dreamy world every now and then. But even in those brief moments when all is well

---

[84] *Midrash Shir Ha'Shirim Rabbah* 1:11
[85] Song of Songs 2:7 and 3:5
[86] Isaiah 64:3

The Invitation

it is not too long before we flare up with worry about what could happen, what could interrupt the tranquility of the moment, or what struggles, financially, health or otherwise, loom ahead of us. That is why all attempts at creating Utopias here and now have failed abysmally. Anything can happen at any moment to shatter the bliss, to disrupt the temporary bubble of our fleeting encounters with our personal or collective Utopian dream. In the Judaic tradition, for example, we believe in perfect faith that there will one day be a new world in which all of Earth's creatures will be gifted with the opportunity to experience lifetimes of total and unimpeded bliss. It will be the ultimate invitation to the ultimate moment. In that time, God will erase tears of sadness, and the way in which we experience death – as tragic -- shall be swallowed-up forever.[87] The lion shall then lay peacefully alongside the calf, the wolf with the lamb, the leopard with the kid-goat, predator with prey, and the young child shall play safely under a nest of killer bees,[88] and nation shall not lift up sword against nation nor shall they learn or teach war anymore.[89]

Yet, as powerful and as staunch as this belief is in the creed of Jewish tradition, the most important, most ancient and most fundamental spiritual and foundational Scriptural directive of the Jewish people, the תורה Torah (literally: "The Guiding"), makes absolutely no mention of any of this, and leaves the dream of tomorrow to the prophets, none of whom so much as attempted to propose a specified **time** for this future reality to occur. They simply referred to their visions as "It shall come to pass in those days" – period.

The Torah, too, in its lengthy narrative recounting the exodus of the Jewish people out of their enslavement in Egypt and their subsequent forty-year journey back to their ancestral homeland, deliberately leaves the reader hanging by concluding the story not with the people's ultimate arrival in their homeland but with the people's **almost** arrival – abandoning the reader on the eastern shores of the Jordan River.[90] In the

---

[87] Isaiah 25:8
[88] Isaiah 11:6-8
[89] Isaiah 2:4
[90] Deuteronomy 1:1

Miriam Maron, BSN, RN, MA, PhD and Gershon Winkler, PhD

Jewish autumn celebrations, this final, seemingly-unfinished segment of the Torah is ritually read to the public from a scroll of the Torah, followed immediately with the reading – out of a second scroll – of the Creation story of Genesis. In other words, we barely make it to where we almost are at the end, when we start all over again. Or, said differently, we ritually practice the dance of Moment, by reading our story in such a manner as to drive home the nature of the dynamics of Life and Death, the realization that endings are but portals to beginnings.

Yes, mortals will continue their attempt, while in this world, to emulate that dreamed-of world that is yet to come, but it is futile and anticlimactic. The main dish at wedding receptions, for example, continues to prove less delightful than the pre-dinner smorgasbord, than the mouth-watering and varied delicacies of the pre-banquet buffet. The Torah takes us only as far as the willow shores of Moab on the eastern banks of the Jordan, and does not take us across the river. We cannot replicate in this realm what is in the next realm. We need to wait for the invitation. And it is not here yet. Over and over again, many have attempted to reconstruct it, to replicate it, to compel it, which has led to centuries of indescribably terrifying cruelty and global calamity. When the ripe time comes, when the invitation is extended, the main dish will prove tastier than the appetizer. Trying to hasten the time is like what we did in the Garden of Eden or in the Desert of Sinai, and will only conjure yet another Golden Calf.

CHAPTER THREE

The Tent of Chosen Time

> **In the space of mystery, God hovered over me as my tent.**[91]

About 3,400 years ago, approximately two-and-a-half million women, men, and children – along with numerous herds of varied livestock – traversed the rocky, sandy wilderness of Sinai. Behind them, memories of centuries of cultural alienation, emotional oppression and forced labor; ahead of them, nothing but Promise, nothing but Uncertainty, nothing but Possibility. The seemingly endless vistas of the seemingly boundless wilderness yielded little more than perpetual fear and anxiety about the Unknown, the Unpredictable. And all their leaders could offer them was a mirage of ideas and imagery about what the elusive and mysterious Next would bring them. They were going home. But it was a home they had never known except through stories about their ancestors. They were headed toward a land they had known only by way of dream and imagination, a land even their leaders and guides, Moses, Miriam and Aaron,[92] had never seen, and never **would** see in their lifetime.

The ancient Hebraic Scriptural narrative of the forty-year journey of the Israelites from the Land of Egypt to the Land of Canaan is a remarkable one in that it occupies four-fifths of the Torah, Judaism's most ancient and most sacred spiritual guide. The message is beyond

---

[91] Job 29:4
[92] Micah 6:4

clear: it's all about the journey. Arriving at the ultimate destination is deliberately absent from this narrative. As mentioned earlier, the story of the Exodus only takes us as far as the eastern shores of the Jordan River. The Torah is not interested in the **getting** there, only in the **going** there. It is the story not only about a particular people's arduous journey from the narrows of constriction to the expanses of liberation, but as much the story of **your** journey across the mysterious chasm of the here-and-now, with all of its promises, all of its randomness, all of its unknowns, all of its uncertainties and all of its possibilities. It is the story of your own anxieties about the mysterious and elusive Next waiting around the corner of your own life walk. Like the ancient Israelites, you carry with you always the conviction of your plans and objectives alongside its ambiguity. Your calendar is amply marked with indications that you will be alive next week, next month, next year, and deep inside you also know that anything can happen at any moment to challenge this assurance and render it null and void. Your calendar holds only your hope, your wish, your assumption; but it cannot hold the reality of chance and the invitation of Moment.

Like the story of the ancient Israelites, your every step is one of Life and Death, of the possibility of both. You see, the Israelites carried with them two arks, two containers, throughout their forty-year trek toward the Promise. One ark carried that which once embodied spirit, and the other ark carried that which continued to inspirit body; one transported the dead remains of their patriarch (Joseph) – and the other transported the Living Breath of their God. The two journeyed side-by-side, often rousing the curiosity of passing Bedouins who would inquire about the contents of the mysterious arks.[93]

> "This one carries the Life-Breath of our God," the Israelites would explain, "and this one carries the remains of a dead man."
>
> "What!? Is it respectful to your God to accompany His ark with that of a corpse?"

---

[93] *Talmud Bav'li, Sotah* 13a-b

"Yes, for these remains are of one who lived-out the intent of our God."

The ark that transported the Divine Presence, or Spirit, was the central focal point of what in Hebrew is called משכן *Mish'kahn*, literally: "That which conjures the Dwelling." Basically, it was a set of five sacred implements that jointly created a mystical space which in turn invoked the Earthly encounter of Creator's Spirit with Creation's Embodiment, or in the language of the sixteenth-century spiritual leader of Gaza, Rabbi Yisrael ben Moshe: "the space within which occurred the joyful unification of Spirit and Body."[94] The five sacred implements were: the Ark of the Covenant, the Altar, the Menorah, the Table of the Facing Bread, and the Copper Basin.

The human animal, too, is an intriguing composite of five basic stratums, each designed to contribute to the cryptic whole of the Divine Intent for what Life and being Human is all about. The five layers of the Human, and the cryptic wisdom represented by each, was thus replicated in this collective arts-and-crafts project that was the *Mishkahn*. The great questions around the "meaning of life" and the "purpose of existence" was encrypted within this magnificent conglomerate of gold, silver, copper, wood and fabric no less than in the human's conglomerate of skin, tissue, arteries, organs, and bones. In fact, what we refer to as Soul, or Consciousness, is embodied by these layers, housed deep within each one of them in very distinct ways, layer within layer within layer, respectively, so that there is an aspect of your soul that lives in and through your body, mind and spirit as follows:

נֶפֶשׁ *nefesh* (your physical Self)
רוּחַ *ru'ach* (your emotive Self)
נְשָׁמָה *neshamah* (your conscious Self)
חַיָה *chayah* (your existential Self)
יְחִידָה *ye'chee'dah* (your cosmic Self)

---

[94] *Shabbat Zemirot, Yah Ree'bon O'lam*

During periods of encampment, the *Mishkahn* was housed in a special tent that was called אהל מועד -- *O'hel Mo'eyd* -- literally: "Tent of Season." Or, in other words: "The Tent of Chosen Time." The Space of the Intersection of Macrocosmic and Microcosmic Journeys. *Mo'eyd* also translates as "Meeting," "Assembly," and "Testimony." It is the activation, or reawakening of the meeting of moment and consciousness, and it is the activation of the many diverse parts within us and outside of us that, when joined, when assembled, brings to life the drama of Creator's Presence in Creation's Unfolding.

The narrative around the construction of this omnipotent, spiritually-infused body of sacred implements makes it clear that it was not some sort of extraterrestrial or Divinely-influenced energy that transformed this otherwise purely material conglomerate into a supernatural force-field. Rather, it was the people. And not only the highly-skilled and spiritually-evolved women and men who participated in its actual construction, but as well the downhome folk whose only involvement was their contribution of material. Because the sole qualification for the privilege of partaking in this momentous endeavor, the Torah recounts, was נדיב לב *ne'deev ley'v*, literally: "a selflessly giving heart."[95] Altruism is the act of moving oneself beyond the bounds of purely subjective desire, want, agenda and impulse to facilitate or create space for the flourishing of Other. *Ne'deev ley'v* is what it takes to tend to the dying as well as the dead, the latter considered in Judaism as the highest form of altruism since the *ne'deev ley'v* receives no expression of gratitude from the dead, and thus the act is completely selfless. It is likened also to the one who gives but knows not to whom she is giving, nor does the recipient know from whom he is receiving.[96] And so does this quality apply also to those who dedicate their time and energies to ביקור חולים *bikur cho'lim*, the benevolent act of tending to, or visiting, those who are ill.[97]

It is this quality of transcendence beyond the finite nature of the physical that in turn forged a spatial infrastructure capable of drawing

---

[95] Exodus 5:21-29

[96] *Talmud Bav'li, Baba Bat'ra* 10b

[97] *Talmud Bav'li, Baba Kama* 100a

upon the spiritual forces and energies of the Beyond. The request that was channeled from Creator in regards to its construction was worded accordingly: "And they shall make for me a מקדש *Mik'dash* [that which will enable the harmonious interplay of Spirit within the realm of Matter], and I shall in turn make my abode in their midst."[98] The implements and all of the material that went into creating the *Mishkahn* represented those very Earthly actions and choices that unify Spirit with Matter, Soul with Body, Creator with Creation. The *Mishkahn*, then, was basically built out of those intentions of the people that were congruent with, that mirrored, the intent of Creator, which was "Creation of Space within Self for the Possibility of Other." This, the ancient mystics taught, was how the universe emerged from out of nothing into the something that it became. It emerged by virtue of the Infinite-All pulling itself inward, as in self-constricting, so to speak, in order to enable the emergence of a space absent of itself within which Creation of Other would be possible, a theory they called *tzimtzum* צמצום, "constriction."

In instructing the ancient Israelites to create the *Mishkahn*, God was then teaching them the mystery of Genesis and that, encrypted within this mystery are clues to the Divine Intent for Creation and the life wisdom necessary for a life walk congruent with that intent. The *Mishkahn* was therefore constructed in such a way as to remain always portable, always in flux and always prepared for travel, for continuous movement. Even in later times, when the *Mishkahn* was eventually housed in a solidly-built permanently constructed and lavishly designed Temple in Jerusalem, it still retained its carrying poles, which were never removed in order to remind the people that the seeming permanence of things is just that -- seeming – but that life is an ongoing journey, and that our journey will be more smooth if we infuse it with flexibility and temporariness.

The mobile, nomadic nature of life was symbolized by the Tent of Chosen Time, of Season, as season is about designated moments, moments that are assigned specific significance and symbolism. These

---

[98] Exodus 25:8

moments are like markers along our lifetime journey. The tent was called by this name because every time the people stopped to camp, the event was marked by this tent being set up, at which time all of the contents of the *Mishkahn* were then gathered within it so that it became a marker of chosen time, an Invitation of the Moment. Tent, after all, unlike a house, represents temporariness and mobility. It was at the same time separate from the *Mishkahn* and an integral part of it. Its original Hebrew name, **אהל מועד** *O'hel Mo'eyd*, also implies "Tent of Assembly," for it was indeed a space for the meeting of the forces of both Heaven and Earth. As such it represented and reminded the people that the endeavor of togetherness and unity is the antithesis to the primal nature of the otherwise ever-expanding universe. The expanding nature of the universe, in its inertial movement outward from within itself – set into motion at the beginning of Creation by God's self-constriction – requires just as much its reversal back toward its central point of Genesis no less than does an exhale require in turn an inhale at some point in order to facilitate continuity. Therefore, taught the ancient rabbis, every time people gather together in love and harmony, whether communally or between friends and lovers, the *Mishkahn* is in those moments re-created, and the scattered sparks of the Light of Creation in turn reverse their movement away from the Divine-All back toward the Point of Beginning, and the universe takes a well-needed deep breath inward, and the Presence of Creator is once more encountered and experienced in the heart of Creation.[99]

The power of Sacred Assembly, or *Mo'eyd*, cannot be underestimated, whether it is a momentary loving glance between two lovers or between parent and child, or a community working in harmony. It is the Big Bang in reverse. It is the necessary inhale of an ever-exhaling existence. The energy that emerges becomes a thread that unifies all of what has become dismembered, by what the mystics referred to as the "Shattering of the Vessels," the inevitable implosion of the primordial universe in its inability to contain the overwhelming newness of its own Genesis. All of us have at one time experienced this personally, the inability to

---

[99] *Talmud Bav'li, Sotah* 17a; *Mishnah, Avot* 3:2

"contain" ourselves, meaning to contain the overwhelming nature of an ecstatic experience or mind-blowing news, a son or daughter getting married or having a baby, a winning lottery ticket, and so on. The antidote to the implosion and inner disconnect in such moments of wanting and needing to connect, is a series of deep inhales.

The gravitational pull of universal interconnectedness is always there, people continue to need one another, be drawn to one another, to be pulled toward and into the Tent of Chosen Time, into the tent of meeting whose energy wove a mystical thread that forged a singular fabric capable of maintaining the diverseness of the twelve tribes within the unit of Israel. The expanding nature of the universe, after all, nevertheless originally emanated from within a single, unified point of beginning.[100] Likewise, while the *Mishkahn* was comprised of various separate entities, each one standing on its own and within its own space and sculpted into its own unique shape, it was the **tent** that unified these diverse parts into a singular sacred whole, transforming those diverse parts into a distinct unit. The lesson was this: Although no one and nothing is essentially the same, everyone and everything is essentially one. When we lose sight of this important universal principle, we create space not for Genesis but for Nemesis. Wrongness, the ancient mystics taught, is enabled when we forget our connectedness to the One, when we forget the singular thread that holds it all together, particularly when the forces of the Masculine and the Feminine are polarized and disconnected from one another.[101] This was the meaning underlying the sacrificial rites, symbolic of the commitment to reunite Heaven and Earth, the Feminine with the Masculine, in the sense of that which represents the raw seeds of dormancy and potential in Creation (the Masculine) uniting with that which endeavors to lovingly evolve those seeds toward their fruition (the Feminine). When the two are disconnected, Creation comes to a standstill and the resulting vacuum becomes a potential arena for the proliferation of wrongness.

---

[100] Zohar, Vol. 1, folio 16b
[101] Zohar, Vol. 1, folio 206b

The Tent of Chosen Time served the important purpose of establishing periodic reminders that the *Mishkahn*, the sacred space of Divine Presence, was not what it was thought to be without the unification, the assemblage, of all of its diverse parts within the single space of the Tent; that the *Mishkahn* – this miniature model of the existential mysteries of the universe – could as easily distort that very same mystery if any one of its parts was to be reckoned absent its connection to the whole of its parts. This is no less a truth involving our physical bodies.

> If one of our hands one day decided not to cooperate with the other hand, we could not build anything, nor could we eat. If our legs tired of being apart all the time and chose instead to unite, we would fall. All exists by cooperation, by each valuing its respective contribution to the whole of life to which all are connected, and each honoring the preciousness of the other as well.[102]

In the Book of Job, for example, Job, who suffers excruciatingly with illness and loss, is desperately trying to understand the meaning of his suffering and what he ever did to deserve it. For thirty-seven chapters of this ancient writ, he and his friends grapple intensely with the question, each taking turns to pontificate personal as well as theological perspectives in a meager attempt to answer the unanswerable. Eventually, toward the very end of the story, Job becomes healed of all his maladies, and everything and everyone he lost is restored to him manifold. Was it a vitamin? A drug? An article he read? Not at all. Rather, it was the act of reversing the "disconnect" that had thrown him into oblivion, into what is referred to throughout the Hebraic scriptures as שאול *Sh'ol*, basically a state of Self-absent-Other. It is from deep within the heart of the churning "whirlwind" of Job's oblivion that God finally reached out to him. And rather than resolve Job's questions with some better solutions than his friends had come up with, God helped Job to **lose** the questions altogether by guiding him out of his "disconnect" mode, coaxing him out of his fixation, and doing so just enough so that he

---

[102] 17th-century Rabbi Eliyahu Ha'Itamri in *Shey'vet Mussar*, Ch. 37

was moved to pray for the well-being of others, moved to shift into a "connect" mode. It was only **then** that he became healed, and only **then** that all that he had lost was restored to him.[103]

Job becomes healed not because of any miraculous action on God's part, but by virtue of stepping outside of the narrow confines of his painful situation into the more expansive horizons of "Life Beyond and in Spite Of Job." In other words, what is restored for Job, what he had lost to begin with -- what it was that had left him so deeply embedded in his suffering -- was the inner joy that stems from the Bigger Picture of Life beyond himself. As Job remarked to God in the aftermath: "All this time, my ears have **heard** you, but now I actually **see** you with my eyes."[104] This is a declaration of his having removed himself from being locked-up inside of himself and having instead emerged beyond himself to the world, to life, outside of the **part** of the whole that was Job to the **whole** of the part that, too, was Job. "Seeing" is a metaphor for **ex**ternalizing, whereas "hearing" is a metaphor for **in**ternalizing. Seeing takes us out of our personal space and connects us with, again, the Bigger Picture.

We must remember, however, that separateness is an illusion. Nothing is truly separate. All are intertwined, each in its unique selfhood, each representing an essential piece of the cosmic puzzle without which the entire scheme would collapse into obscurity. This was the message of the Menorah, the golden, seven-branched candelabra that illuminated the sacred space of the *Mishkahn*. Modeled pretty much after the Moriah sagebrush indigenous to the Sinai wilderness, it was shaped like a stem with six branches, three on each side, the central stem representing the seventh. Yet, with all of its symbolic implications of diversity by way of its distinct and separate branches, all of its varied components had to be carved out of a single chunk of gold.[105] In other words, as fragmented and as differentiated as everyday life might feel to us, our sense of that separation is but the way in which we **experience** it,

---

[103] Job 42:10
[104] Job 42:5
[105] Exodus 25:36

the way in which we choose to **define** it, and by the actions that result from those choices. But in essence it is all a single chunk of existence comprised of many branches, many avenues, all leading away from – yet back to – the oneness that it is. It is our work in the world to seek out, in everything that we do, the central column of the Menorah out of which we branch in so many diverse ways and within which we nonetheless remain rooted.

Mishkahn משכן is one word. By itself, it defines nothing and means nothing. It takes on purpose only because of the diverse parts of which it is comprised. The table, or שולחן *shul'chahn* with the Show-Bread – the לחם הפנים *le'chem ha'pa'neem* -- represents your bodily self, your נפש *nefesh*, the part of you that is incomplete, that needs and wants; that lusts and hungers, longs and thirsts. It was therefore situated in the direction of North, or, in Hebrew צפון *tsa'fon*, literally: "Hidden-Away," as in "Preserved" for the purpose of becoming revealed at a later time. North is then symbolic of incompleteness and mystery. After all, is that not what mystery is really about? Something missing? When something is missing, we can see it as either lacking, as in defective, or as infinite possibility, as in yet more to come. "Why did God leave the North incomplete?" asked the ancient rabbis. "So that if anyone claims to be a god," they quipped, "let them come forward and finish the North."[106] In other words, anyone claiming to be Divine, let them come forward and so much as attempt to decode the cryptic secrets of Creation, to unlock the mystery of Existence. This sense of "incompleteness" is important also in the sense that it reminds us not to lock ourselves into the definitive, to always leave space for possibility, for something other than what we presume to be "it" in all matters. The bread on this "show" table, baked fresh weekly, demonstrated exactly this lesson. Bread, as wheat grass alchemized to fruition, is mystery revealed, but not completely, because the possibilities of its fruition do not end with bread alone. All revelation of mystery, then, remains forever incomplete, even **Divine** revelation.[107] The body, like the Earth

---

[106] *Midrash Pirkei D'Rebbe Eliezer*, Ch. 3
[107] *Midrash Bereisheet Rabbah* 17:5

herself, while seemingly very vividly and dramatically revealed to our eyes, is pure mystery. Everything is far more than it seems, and is but an expression of selective revelation. What it shows you is only what it **chooses** to show you, no less than how you appear to others reveals only the face you choose to show in that moment. The Show-Bread, in its original Hebrew, was therefore appropriately called לחם הפנים *le'chem ha'pa'neem*, literally: "Bread of the Faces." The physical universe, in other words, is a disguise which camouflages deep mystery, revealing aspects of itself as determined by choice and moment. This is why one of the words in Hebrew for our universe is עולם *o'lahm*, which literally translates as: "Hidden," the implication being that Creator is hidden within Creation, within the universe,[108] and reveals of itself only what it chooses, and only **when** it chooses. Not much different from any one of **us**.

The Menorah, on the other hand, represents your passionate, **feeling** self, your רוח *ru'ach*. Accordingly, it was situated in the direction of South, the place of cleared space. South in Hebrew is נגב *negev*, literally: "wiped clean," precisely what you need to work at to arrive at the core truth of what exactly it is that you are feeling in any given moment in response to any given situation. Your feelings, though they stem from the single entity that you are, nonetheless tend to branch-out into many, and often conflicting, sensations. All of these branches, the Menorah reminds you, must be kindled from the unifying flame of the Central Column, the trunk of the tree, the central core of who you are in essence. And to do so requires the quality of South, of *negev*, the act of wiping the slate clean of all its noise and rabble, retracing your steps from the deafening roar of the waterfall of circumstance all the way upstream to the calm of the gently oozing trickle of the hidden wellspring out of which it emerges. The word מנורה "Menorah" literally means "That which illuminates," as in that power within you that enables you to discover clarity, to illuminate the murkiness and delineate the blur of your multitudes of feelings about any given encounter.

---

[108] Jeremiah 23:24; *Bahir*, Ch. 10; *Midrash D'varim Rabah* 2:26

The copper wash basin, or **כיור נחושת** *kee'yor ne'cho'shet*, represents your aware self, your cognitive, thinking, reasoning self, your **נשמה** *neshamah*. It was located in the direction of West, or in Hebrew **מערב** *ma'arav*, literally: "That Which Blends," as West is where day blends into night, light into darkness. Water, too, is the force of blending, the unifying element that conjures within all diverse entities their common core, which in turn enables integration and unification. This is what you do in your head, in your *neshamah* place. It is there that you synthesize your thoughts and your feelings toward a unified knowing and understanding, choice and determination. The ritual of rinsing oneself in the waters of the copper wash basin prior to entering the Holy of Holies represented this quality of preparation that is asked of you prior to you rendering a decision or performing an action. All that emerges, emerges from behind the veil of Water: "And *Elo'heem* said, 'The waters that are beneath the heavens should now gather to the place of unification, so that the dry land might become revealed.'"[109]

The altar, or **מזבח** *meez'bay'ach*, was situated in the direction of East, or in Hebrew **מזרח** *meez'rach*, literally: "That Which Radiates," as in the direction out of which the sun first begins to shine. It is also called **קדם** *kedem* for that very reason, literally: "Beginning," as in the direction out of which the day begins. This is the part of you that awakens your sense of your Aliveness, your **חיה** *chayyah*, the inner joy of simply Being, the ecstasy of a moment – even just a short-lived burp of a moment -- when nothing is hurting and nothing is wrong, and you have no sense whatsoever of the tumultuousness of your everyday concerns, only of your existence and the pure bliss of it. You are the altar, upon which all else is in that moment sacrificed, offered-up in pure joy as an acknowledgment to Creator that all originates with, is sustained by, and returns to, the One that is the All.

The Ark of the Covenant, or **ארון הברית** *a'ron ha'breet*, represents your unified self, your **יחידה** *ye'chee'dah*, that part of you that in essence is one with everything that is and with everything that is not. This is your most essential Self that is primarily unknown to you

---

[109] Genesis 1:9

since it streams forth from "what is impossible for the mouth to speak and for the ear to hear."[110] It is no wonder that one could not simply approach the Ark of the Covenant without risking being zapped into non-existence, for it represented the demarcation of what is and what is not, of where Creator and Creation became completely merged yet at the same time totally separate. Once you become again one with God, in other words, you are no longer a part of God, nor are you God. You are neither. Rather, you are, again, "what is impossible for the mouth to speak and for the ear to hear." So don't go there. And those who did, vanished.

The Ark of the Covenant stood in the center, in the Heart of the *Mishkahn*. It was the unifying force that held all of its parts together while preserving the distinct and individual uniqueness of each component. It represented the gravitational pull of all separate parts in their respective orbit within and around the whole that, together, they comprised. It is symbolic of the mystery that binds together all of the distinct molecules that make up who and what you are. That is the nature of "covenant." Within this mystical ark sat the tablets of the original Ten Commandments which Moses had shattered in reaction to the Golden Calf fiasco, as well as the second set of tablets he was instructed by God to prepare for the rewrite. The first set of stones had been fashioned **and** written by God itself.[111] The second set of stones that God re-wrote was prepared by Moses.[112] The Ark of the Covenant, and thus the meaning implied by "covenant," was then about the capacity to hold both in unison, hope and betrayal, wholeness and brokenness, the brokenness of Divine Revelation and the wholeness of human imperfection. This is the part of you that **gets** all of this, yet doesn't. This is the part of you that knows the deepest mystery of mysteries, yet has no clue what it is. It is the story of Moses who communicates with God "face to face,"[113] yet begs God to show Itself to him.[114] The Ark of the Covenant held

---

[110] *Talmud Yerushalmi, Nedarim* 9a
[111] Exodus 32:16
[112] Exodus 34:1
[113] Exodus 33:11
[114] Exodus 3:18

the Presence of the God Who is nowhere and everywhere, and who is simultaneously סתים וגליא *sa'teem v'gal'ya* -- "hidden and revealed."[115]

In this very moment as you read these words, you are a sacred space, a *Mishkahn*, within which Creation is unfolding in all of its known and unknown characteristics. You are an activated embodiment of the Divine Intent that moves existence into being and becoming. Every physical embodiment of that intent – whether rock, plant, or animal – receives this intent in accordance with its particular capacity to contain and manifest and facilitate the pulsating force of the Divine Presence, of the God Breath. However, due to the finite nature of the physical, we can only embody the moment, we can only embody the various phases of the Divine Intent for Creation in "Seasons," in "Chosen Times." And so, Genesis happens all over again, repeatedly, by way of the "Shattering of the Vessels," the cracking of the shells, out of which new worlds emerge. As we read in the Talmud: "God created worlds and destroyed worlds, created worlds and destroyed worlds, until this one came about."[116] The illusion of separateness is the reality of the Big Bang and the ever-expanding – or separating – universe. The act of assemblage, on the other hand, as dramatized by the Tent of Meeting, the Tent of Chosen Time, is the act of transcending that illusion by reconnecting what has come apart, bringing near what has become distanced, and putting Humpty-Dumpty back together again. In those moments, when we move selflessly out of the separateness of Self to reach out toward the uniqueness of Other, our **own** disconnected parts come that much closer together, and the uniqueness of our own Selfhood becomes that much more apparent, and we become then the Tent of Chosen Time, of the Invitation of the Moment, and of Meeting, of unification. It is in those actions that the *Mishkahn* within us becomes activated. Because, as the Torah clearly implies, the *Mishkahn* itself, with all of its sacred implements and their inherent spiritual potencies, still required activation. In order for the Presence of **Creator** to be pronounced, the presence of **Creation** needed to be pronounced as well. Even though

---

[115] Zohar, Vol. 1, folio 39b
[116] *Midrash Bereisheet Rabbah* 3:7

the *Mishkahn* had been completed to perfection, it remained lifeless and moot until Moses performed the rites of activation: "And Moses 'raised-up' the *Mishkahn*."[117] The *Mishkahn* still required the act of infusing the intent of the people into that which now held the intent of God, thus triggering the electrical charge of both, the forces of Heaven and the forces of Earth, the energies of the Masculine and the energies of the Feminine, creating the kiss of Spirit and Matter.

This powerful place, this traveling vortex of the dance of Spirit and Matter, became from then on a living aggregate of the interrelationship and dynamics between Soul and Body. When the Presence of Spirit filled the tent, no one, not even Moses, could enter, and when it lifted, its ascension implied a chosen time during which space was enabled for Other, for the presence of physical embodiment. It represented the paradox of unification, the paradox of intimacy, that intimacy in its purest definition was not about exclusive focus on unification absent separateness, but, on the contrary, it was about unification **accompanied** by separateness, so that neither party would lose their precious Selfhood in the **blur** of Other but rather **discover** their precious Selfhood in the **clarity** of Other. The tragic death of the two sons of Moses' brother Aaron, who was the High Priest of the nation, may have been the result of their failure to realize this very important truth. In their haste to become one with Spirit, they indeed succeeded in doing exactly that,[118] and in the process lost their Selfhood, their unique, separate Life Force, in the blur of Other, that Other being Spirit. The rituals articulated to the people around the science of unification with Spirit had clearly emphasized the importance of maintaining and respecting separateness in all endeavors of connectedness; that, again, we are all indeed One, but not the Same.

Life is to Death as the Body is to the Soul, as Moses was to the Tent. We know that in Life we walk side-by-side with Death, and that it is a matter of time for all of us. We journey through our own individual wilderness carrying the inevitable with us, carrying both the Ark of

---

[117] Exodus 40:18
[118] Leviticus 10:1-2

the Covenant -- of that which fuses Body and Soul into a single entity, into a single persona -- and the Ark of Death. We also carry the Tent of Chosen Time, the portal, the gateway through which we will one day transition into the realm of Spirit. It is where we invest our actions, our intentions, and our choices, bringing to it all that we are when the time is chosen for us to enter. Our task is to not **rush** the chosen time for the Death that will one day embrace us, but to gift Death with the space to be what it is in its own right and to reach out to us when the time of the "meeting" is chosen, when the Invitation arrives. In this way, we can enjoy a more spatial relationship with Death while in Life, where we give Death its space, and Death in turn gives us our space to live a fuller Life.

The Tent of Chosen Time is your persona, the sum total of both your physical and spiritual Self. Just as the five essential implements of the *Mishkahn* were housed within the Tent, likewise are the five layers of your soul housed within your persona. Your persona is far more than your skin, than your outer appearance, no less than the Tent was far more than the outer appearance of the *Mishkahn*. You entered that Tent at a specifically chosen time, the time chosen for you to be born into this lifetime. And you will one day leave the Tent when the Spirit alights upon it, when the One who gave you, chooses to take you. In the Wilderness of Sinai, the times chosen for journeying, as well as for setting up camp, was determined by the drama of the Presence of Spirit within the Tent. When it descended upon the Tent, it was time to set up camp, and when it ascended, it was time to resume the journey.[119] In a similar manner, when your soul descended within your body, it became the time chosen for you to set up camp, to be in Life. And when one day your soul will depart from your body, it will be indicative of the time chosen for you to pack up and resume your journey.

> In the twilight of my days I will walk within the very gates of the underworld; I have been recalled from the remainder of my years. I said, "I will not see Yah" – Yah in the Land of the Living, that is; I will no longer gaze upon humanity, along with the rest of

---

[119] Exodus 40:34-37

the earth's inhabitants. My earthly dwelling has been lifted, and carried away from me like a shepherd's tent.[120]

The Tent is both, a portal to the Next, a gateway to the Unknown, and the very persona that you have evolved across the span of your lifetimes. It is the sacred space within which you and the One Who Called You into Becoming meet at chosen times, and where the electrical charges of your intimate connection become renewed. It is where you return to begin so that you might begin to return. This moment, right now, is an opportunity for you to practice this by doing whatever good you're doing in a way that you've never done it before. In this way, you will avoid flat-lining your eternal journey and instead be ever-spiraling. "In a way," wrote Rabbi Abraham Joshua Heschel, "death is the test of the meaning of life. If death is devoid of meaning, then life is absurd."[121]

Living a meaningful death therefore requires us to do now what it is we wish to manifest tomorrow. The long-hoped-for Utopian dream of the Messianic times, when everything will be okay and all conflict resolved and all hurt healed -- will only continue to follow us to the grave unless we make the effort of contributing what we can of our little selves to make it a reality in the short but opportune time of our sojourn on Earth. The famous Ghandi adage "Become yourself the very change you wish to see in the world" was long ago instilled into the ideological fabric of the Jewish nation and more so into its daily ritual practice, a practice intended to gently move our behavior from one of subjective impulse and possessiveness to one of conscientious reflection and altruism. This is a delicate dance of Self and Other, of separateness and connectedness, of maintaining awareness of the uniqueness of Self while at the same time maintaining awareness of the uniqueness of Other. This very fundamental principle of the Judaic wisdom path is encrypted within the most hallowed mantra repeated by Jewish people worldwide to this very day: The *Shema*. First introduced more than 3,300 years ago by Moses, and addressed to the Israelites, the words are:

שמע ישראל י-ה-ו-ה אלהינו י-ה-ו-ה אחד

---

[120] Isaiah 38:10-12

[121] *Reflections on Death* [Farrar, Straus, and Giraux]

Listen **deeply**, O Israelites; *yhwh* [The Un-Nameable Unknowable, Undefinable Mover of All Existence] is our God; *yhwh* is **Only** [and therefore inclusive of all and every]."[122] The common belief by many that this mantra is Judaism's declaration of its monotheistic creed weakens its far broader message. God is not "one" but, more clearly said: God is "only." **One** is a number, and as such, it exists solely by virtue of its relationship to **other** numbers, without which it does not exist as the one that it purports to be. Rather, and more accurately translated, the reference to the Oneness of God, as rendered in the original Hebrew -- אחד *e'chad* – implies "Only."[123] And if God is Only, it follows that everyone and everything is interconnected, emanating from, enlivened by, made possible by, enabled by and integrally woven within, The **Only**. The Mosaic Mantra then reads like this: "Listen deeply, O Israel, *yhwh* is **our** God, our very personal God with whom we are learning to enjoy a very intimate relationship that is uniquely ours. But at the same time it is imperative that you remember that *yhwh* is **Only**, and therefore incorporative of **all** that exists, and thus equally in relationship with all **others**, each in a way that is unique to **them**."

The idea of a God who is at the same time our personal God while also the God of everyone else is a challenge to the subjective-oriented nature of the human animal who would like to presume that everything belongs to him or her and that she or he is the most deserving creature on the planet. Periodically, the ancient Hebrew prophets would reiterate this separate, universal attribute of God to a people for whom God was at the same time being taught as personal and private:

> In that day shall Israel be third alongside Egypt and Assyria, as a blessing on Earth; for God will bless them, saying: "Blessed is my people Egypt, my handiwork Assyria, and my inheritance Israel."[124]

---

[122] Deuteronomy 6:4
[123] Maharal in *Netivot Olam, Vol. 1, Netiv Ha'Avodah*, Ch. 7, folio 99
[124] Isaiah 19:24

Are you not just like the Children of the Ethiopians unto me, O Children of Israel? Did I not bring out Israel from the Land of Egypt, but also the Philistines from out of Caf'tor, and Aram from out of Kir?"[125]

It is written, "There never again arose among the Israelites a prophet as great as Moses" (Deuteronomy 34:10) – indeed, among the Israelites there never again arose a prophet as great as Moses, but amongst other peoples, there **did** arise."[126]

Martin Buber put it this way: "As a historical people, Israel enjoys no precedence over any other. Like Israel, the other peoples were all wanderers and settlers; they came 'up' from a land of want and servitude into their present homeland. The one God, the Redeemer and Leader of the peoples, strode before all of them upon their way -- even the hostile neighboring peoples -- protecting them by His might. He guided their steps, gave them power, let them 'inherit' the soil of a people that had been ruined by its sins and abandoned by history."[127]

The honoring of the importance of both relationships, near and distant, intimate but separate, became deeply threaded within the evolution of this ancient wisdom which, although prevalent in the life walk of the earlier Hebrew ancestors centuries before, in the Wilderness Journey it now became more clearly unpacked and delineated for a burgeoning nation of their descendants.

The injunctions of the Torah were revolutionary to the people not only in their introduction of standards of behavior far above the cultural norm of that period (and in some instances even of our own times), but also in their challenge to the people that they endeavor to hold equally in their daily equation of their individual and communal life walk the sanctity of separateness and the sanctity of interconnectedness; the sanctity of the **Doing** time during the week and the sanctity of the **Being** time during the Sabbath; the sanctity of intimacy and the

---

[125] Amos 9:7
[126] *Midrash Bamid'bar Rabbah* 14:19
[127] *Martin Buber on the Bible*, Ed. N. Glatzer [Schocken Books, 1982], p. 80

sanctity of separation; the sanctity of filling what is empty and the sanctity of emptying what is full; the sanctity of Life and the sanctity of Death. It is not surprising then, that, historically, the most important last words on the lips of an Israelite, is the שמע *Shema*. Death is, after all, a moment of separation, and, at the same time, a moment of interconnectedness, of reunification with the One Who is the All, with the One Who, in the same breath, is and is not; with the One Who one day will beckon to each of us from behind the veil of mystery, from within the Tent of Meeting, and extend to us *The Invitation*.

CHAPTER FOUR

The Red Cow

> Have the gates of death been revealed to you? And have you seen the gates of the death-shadow?[128]

Death is the most vivid drama of Life. It isn't until we have encountered Death that Life becomes in that moment more pronounced. At the same time, with the arrival of Death, comes the departure of Life, not only for the dead but for the living as well. What has until that point been taken for granted, Life, suddenly vanishes, and those left behind have in one fell swoop become derailed, abruptly cast asunder from out of the confidence of perpetuity and assurance into the fragility of chance and uncertainty. Because of the potency of the drama of Death and the magnitude of its power to eject us from our life flow, a process of healing is needed to restore in us our displaced sense of the potency of the drama of **Life**.

In ancient times, such a process was guised in a mysterious ritual known as פרה אדומה *parah a'dumah*, literally: Red Cow,[129] an extremely rare phenomenon. Anyone having come into contact with death, whether in battle or by tending to the dead, was not permitted back into the community before undergoing this strange seven-day cleansing ritual. There is in fact no other state of "ritual impurity" treated with so much fanfare in the Torah as that caused by anything

---

[128] Job 38:17
[129] Numbers, Chapter 19

remotely related to Death. Of course, the question which then arises is: If Death is so sacred, as we have studied in earlier chapters, then why require purification altogether? Why is Death considered the highest degree of "ritual impurity" in the Torah?

Ritual "impurity" in the ancient Hebrew is טומאה *tum'ah*, and ritual "purity" is טהרה *taharah*. Both terms have been sadly mistranslated out of their indigenous contexts for ages, to the point that the average person holds *tum'ah* as bad, filthy, "impure", and *taharah* as good, clean, and "pure." Neither definition is anywhere near accurate. Rather, at their root meanings, *tum'ah* stems from the word טום *tum*, which means "to fill up,"[130] and *taharah* stems from the word טהירו *tehee'ru* which implies "cleared space," as in the space God cleared within Itself, within which to create Other,[131] or as in "clear sky."[132] The concept of "purifying the impure" is then about **clearing** a space that has been occupied so **fully** that there would otherwise have been little or no room for permeability, for continuity, for possibility of other than what was or is. When Death occurs in front of us, the drama of it does indeed fill us, and little space if any remains for Life Awareness in that moment. The Red Cow ritual was intended to clear the fog.

Many have attempted to explain the mysterious meanings behind this puzzling ceremony. Many have tried to offer rational explanations, psychological, philosophical, and otherwise, but this particular injunction of the Torah continues nevertheless to elude the most noble of efforts. Part of the reason may be that we are looking for clues in all the wrong places.

In the first century, they asked Rabbi Yochanan ben Zakai about this seemingly obscure ceremony of the Red Cow. He replied, in his usual cryptic style: "[I swear] by your lives! The dead do not contaminate, and the waters do not purify. Rather, thus did the Holy Blessed One say, 'A statute have I instituted; a decree have I declared, and you cannot override it.'"[133] Perhaps more than any other attempt to explain

---

[130] *Talmud Bav'li, Baba Kama* 51b
[131] *Zohar*, Vol. 1, folio 251a
[132] *Talmud Bav'li, Berachot* 51a
[133] *Midrash Pesik'ta D'Rav Kahana* 4:18

Red Cow, Rabbi Yochanan's truncated response articulates it best. He does not delve into all sorts of mystical or psychological possibilities, as we will be doing later in this chapter. Rather, he reminds us of what we have forgotten. He shakes us out of our stupor of predications and assumptions. We presume that vegetables, for example, are good for us because they contain nutrients that are compatible with our biological constitutions in such ways that they nurture us and sustain us. Wrong, says Yochanan son of Zakai. That's the reasoning we come up with based on our own assumptions about how life works and where all the pieces fit. Our reasoning behind why we need air to breathe, or why objects fall toward the earth is based entirely on premises that we have invented over the millennia based on our finite capacity to make sense of things so that 2+2=4. And so we created a body of laws, such as the Laws of Physics, or of Astronomy, or of Biology and Chemistry and Mathematics, and so on. And everything falls into place neatly and squarely.

"By your lives!" admonishes Rabbi Yochanan, "you need to know that it is not so at all. 2+2=4 because God decreed it so. If God wished it, 2+2 would be 5 and we wouldn't even question it, for we would have labeled **that** as the Laws of Mathematics. Substitute "Laws of Nature" or "Laws of Physics" with "Laws of God," and we begin to fathom the depths of Ben Zakai's lesson. Did Newton's apple fall from the tree because of **gravity**, or did the tree **release** it? The effect might be the same, that it lands on the ground below, but the **cause** depends on your worldview. And the worldview being presented here is that the cause is neither. Rather, the apple falls to the ground because God so designed it. It is part of the infrastructural dynamics of how God chose to create the physical universe, and there is not a thing any of us can do to alter it. Or, in the words of Ben Zakai: "Thus did the Holy Blessed One say, 'A statute have I instituted; a decree have I declared, and you cannot override it.'" We can operate within it, we can meander about within its bounds, but we cannot move beyond it. Even God Itself chooses to work within those very same laws that God chose for the existence of physical subsistence.

> Do you think that five and five are ten? But cannot God make five and five twelve? Says Maimonides: No. God Himself is bound up by His own creations and by the reason that permeates these creations.[134]

Notice, for example, how no culture throughout human history has ever come up with a number beyond the number 9. The number 10 is basically the number 1 all over again, albeit on a subsequent plane, but it is not a **new** number. In the Kabbalistic doctrine of the *Ten Sefirot* (Divine Energies that enable and perpetuate existence), the Tenth *Sefirah* does not exist other than as an incorporate quality inclusive of the **Nine** *Sefirot*. The Ten Commandments, too, are actually **Nine**, the first one, "I am the Infinite All," inclusive of the remaining 9 that follow – as in "I am the Infinite All, and therefore…." The ancient rabbis tell us how God created the universe with "Ten Utterances." But if you count them in the first chapter of Genesis ("And God said: 'Let there be this and that…'") you will only find **nine**. The tenth, again, is all-inclusive, it is **1** all over again but enrobed in the quality of incorporation, of unifying the many. The tenth "utterance" the sages were referring to is none other than the unfathomable First Thought out of which existence emerged. It is the "**uni**" behind the "**verse**."

Nothing, then, is essentially and at its core what it seems. Water is what it is and does what it does not because of how we have chosen to understand it but because God intended it so. Period. It may not satisfy our quest for the knowledge of Why and How, but that is what the proverbial story of the Garden of Eden and the Forbidden Fruit is all about. In our haste, we plucked the fruit of knowledge prematurely, before it had a chance to ripen, and we came away therefore with an "incomplete" wisdom about things, a predicament with which we are grappling to this day. The human lust for knowledge, for having to figure everything out, is overwhelming. It eats at us daily. The Forbidden Fruit ate **us** more than we ate **it**. The quest for Why and How consumes us. And all Science can offer is **How**, but never **Why**. Because, **Why** remains concealed within the grasp of the One Who

---

[134] Rabbi Abraham Joshua Heschel in *Moral Grandeur and Spiritual Audacity*, p. 160

Chose to Make it Just ***So***, and no more than we can figure out ourselves can we figure out the mystery behind existence, behind what we glibly refer to as God.

> For My thoughts are not your thoughts, and your ways are not My ways, and as high as are the heavens from the earth, so high are My ways from your ways and My thoughts from your thoughts (Isaiah 55:8-9).

So you want to know the meaning behind the Red Cow ritual, asked Ben Zakai? It is a ritual designed to awaken you from the dead after you have encountered Death. Because Death is more than breathing your last breath. Death is living in the illusion that there is such a thing as Death. Death is not what you have defined it any more than is water what you have defined **it**, or lettuce or salt. Therefore, just as it is not anything in water itself that keeps you alive, but it is the will of God that water acts as the agent to do just that for you, likewise it is not anything in the Red Cow concoction or its ceremony that clears you of the trauma of death, but it is the will of God that this particular blend and its ritual performs that function for you. This is the thrust of Rabbi Yochanan's lesson. Everything is, because it was so intended by the One-Who-Spoke-and-the-World-Came-into-Being. What we do within what **is**, of course remains our choice. But it is what it is, not because of anything we can fathom, our well-meaning stories and theories notwithstanding. It is what it is because it was so "decreed"; it was so established along with all the other non-negotiable laws of nature and the universe.

Having challenged ourselves with Rabbi Yochanan's staggering yet necessary and significant lesson, we can now return to the more cushioned realm of mortal thought and reasoning in exploring the Red Cow ceremony.

When the extremely rare phenomenon of a totally red cow occurred, she was ritually slaughtered on the sacred altar and then completely burned, skin, flesh, blood, entrails, all consumed by fire and reduced to a heap of ashes. A branch from an acacia tree wrapped in crimson-dyed yarn woven by a snail[135] was also thrown into the fire. The combined ashes were then gathered-up and kept outside the community for use in ceremonies directed at those who have had encounters with death. A designated woman[136] or man would gather a measure of these ashes and create this mysterious blend in preparation for the ritual. The כהן Ko'hayn (ritual facilitator) would then sprinkle the mixture on the subject with a hyssop branch. The ceremony then incorporated the dance of Earth (the ashes), Fire, and Water. Earth represents the mystery of life locked into the seed of potential. Water represents the unlocking force that opens the seed of mystery to enable revelation of dormant, concealed potential. And fire represents the force of alchemy that draws the newly-emerging revelation to its fullest blossoming and highest possibility, *a la* the sun, for example.

The Red Cow, in its perfectly unblemished state, was symbolic of *tum'ah*, of fullness, completeness, nowhere else to go, nothing further to do, no space for improvement in the here-and-now realm, and thus representative of death itself. The acacia branch was representative of potential brought to fruition from the plant world, and the yarn (silk?) spun by a snail was representative of potential brought to fruition from the animal world. All this was reduced to their common core essence: Earth (ash), within which the seed of **all** potential fruition is concealed. Once returned to its core essence of mystery by way of fire, water is added for the effect of unlocking the mystery of Genesis afresh. And this potion, with all of its myriad representations in essence and in symbol, is then ritually sprinkled at the individual needing a ceremony to clear out the trauma that now fills him, to clear the *tum'ah*, and bring him to a place of fresh new beginnings, of *taharah*, of fresh new possibilities freed up of the impediments of past. Ritual purification, on whatever level, is then about disassembling what **has** been, in order to create fresh space for what **can** be; for renewal.

The כהן *Ko'hayn* would sprinkle the individual seven times with this mysterious blend, repeating this ritual twice over a seven-day period

---

[135] *Midrash Sif'ra*, 1:14
[136] *Mishnah, Parah* 5:4

of segregation and purification, on the third day and on the seventh day. Thereafter, the individual was permitted re-entry into the community, but the *Ko'hayn* had to remain outside the community for an entire day and night, following which he would immerse himself in a natural gathering of Living Waters, such as a river or a lake, or ritual pool known as מקוה *mikveh*, and only then was he, too, able to return to the community.

The Red Cow ritual is a crucial one. Sadly in our own times we lack such ceremonies for warriors returning from the battle field, or for individuals such as hospital personnel and emergency professionals, whose work involves encounters with death on a regular basis. Instead, soldiers returning from war are ushered straight back into their communities and their homes, bringing with them the trauma and drama of death, which in turn thwarts and often outright **shatters** the life-affirming attributes of family and community. Rituals such as the *Red Cow* were intended to prevent such negative dynamics from contaminating the community and to avert post-traumatic stress syndrome so common in our era.

"Cow" in Hebrew is פר *par*. Etymologically, this ancient word for cow is about "separation," as in moving something above and beyond itself.[137] It therefore appears as a prefix to numerous other words in the Hebrew language that imply separation. Even in herds, cows tend to go their separate ways and stray off on their own. The Red Cow, if and when one was found and designated for this ritual, had to be void of any scars or lesions, no marks or blemishes of any sort, and had to be at least two years old and never subjected to the yoke. In fact, the sages had a way of determining whether the cow had ever had a yoke on its shoulders.[138] Bottom line, the animal had to have had a positive, wholesome experience of living during her two years, never worked a day in her life, meaning that no one had ever benefited any gain from her, and she had never been injured -- a total beneficiary of all that is good and positive in this life. She must be completely red, like blood, the

---

[137] e.g., *Talmud Yerushalmi, Gitin* 32a
[138] *Midrash Pesikta Rabbati* 14:2

color of דין *deen*, of positive Judgment and Precision,[139] which emanates from the left side of the Sefirotic Tree, the great cosmic mystery out of which existence is perpetually sprouting and branching-out into all of its myriad manifestations. She is the carrier of the Divine Luminations that are moving the Life Force into Creation – like sap in tree, and like blood in body – filtered through the Feminine Realm of the Divine Intent, the realm of precision and discernment, the realm of *deen*.

> "And you shall take onto yourself a Red Cow that is Whole and Unblemished, which has never had upon it a yoke."[140] **Red Cow** represents the שכינה *She'chee'nah* [the Feminine Attribute of the Divine Presence in Creation] of the Below [of the earthly realms, emanating] from the side of [the Sefirotic Tree that is] גבורה *Gevurah* [the quality of balancing and tempering the flow of חסד *Chessed*, which in turn is the quality of unrestrained divine gifting]. **Whole** represents the side of *Chessed*, which is the realm that is [archetypally-embodied by the ancestor] Abraham, about whom it is said: "Walk before me and be Whole."[141] **Unblemished** represents the Central Column עמודא דאמצעיתא – *A'mu'da D'amtzu'eeta* – [the perfect undeviating stream of the Divine Will moving from Divine Thought to Divine Manifestation in Creation]. **Which has never had upon it a yoke** represents the *She'chee'nah* of the Above [of the spirit realms], toward which the forces of evil and confusion are incapable of approaching.[142]

In our own times, as well as in ancient times, a milder version of these "purification" rites involves the *mikveh*, the ritual pool, or a lake, river, ocean -- any natural gathering of "living" waters, as in non-seasonal and always flowing. Literally, the word *mikveh* translates as (1) "that which gathers," and (2) "that which brings hope." The ritual of the *mikveh* achieves both: **gathering** for the individual what has been dispersed, what has been scattered or become disconnected amid the

---

[139] Zohar, Vol. 3, folio 180b
[140] Numbers 19:2
[141] Genesis 17:1
[142] Zohar, Vol. 3, folio 180b

trauma or drama of her encounter with death, and restoring **hope** by unblocking what might be stuck, what might have become petrified in time by the encounter.

Death, then, is not "un-**clean**." More accurately, it is "un-**clear**." And when it happens in front of our eyes we are hit in the gut with it, and our sense of life-continuity is interrupted and frozen in time. It is a stirring drama that challenges our security, our sense of the infinite, our assurance concerning tomorrow and the days after. It leaves us shaken and sends us reeling into the darkness of mystery, once again locked into the seed of Genesis from which we had long sprouted forth and from which we had long ago sprung onward. From the blossoming colors of our personal Summer we have been thrown cold-turkey into the Grey of Autumn. And we have become clueless once again, our schooling and academic degrees notwithstanding.

CHAPTER FIVE

Perpetuity

> **All of the rivers, they journey to the sea. Yet, the sea is never full. To the place where the rivers flow, that is where they return to journey.**[143]

Among the most important instructions given to the ancient Israelites during their forty-year desert trek 3,300 years ago, was that of Season; that there are seasons, cycles, phases, in the ever-unfolding drama of our Earthly existence. There is a time to **in**hale and a time to **ex**hale, a time to **do** and a time to **be** – or not. Some of this is built into the design of Nature, such as the seasons of Spring, Summer, Autumn and Winter, and some of it is built into the design of the bigger picture, the Force that moves the wheels of existence from behind the פרגוד *par'gawd*, behind the Veil of the Great Cosmic Mystery. From the ancients we have come to know these cycles in **Sevens**.

Obviously, the number "**7**" is not coincidental. We have the seven phases of Creation in the Genesis story, and, of course, the seventh day of the week -- the Sabbath -- and there are seven weeks between the festival of Passover and that of *Shavu'ot*,[144] between the exodus of the Israelites from Egypt and their arrival at Mount Sinai for the great Revelation. So what is the significance of this number that there were seven cycles or phases of Creation, or that every seventh day is Shabbat,

---

[143] Ecclesiastes 1:7
[144] Leviticus 23:15

or that there are seven colors in the rainbow, or that our ancestor Jacob had to work seven years to earn his marriage to his beloved Rachel[145] and then later bows seven times as he makes his way toward his estranged brother Esau[146] during their reconciliatory reunion? And what about the seven years it took Solomon to construct the First Temple,[147] or the seven branches of the ancient Menorah (candelabra),[148] or the seven blessings traditionally recited at Jewish wedding ceremonies; or the seven rounds to the ancient Jewish willow dance at the conclusion of the harvest celebrations,[149] or that the Hebrew calendar begins its new year in the seventh month,[150] and that there are seven heavens, seven earths (or underworlds),[151] or that three sevens in a row lands you a jackpot in Reno, or that Pharaoh dreamt of seven skinny cows swallowing seven plump cows?[152] And so on… And of course, let's not forget Snow White and the Seven Dwarfs!

So it turns out that the Hebrew word for **Seven**, שבע *sheva*, is an offspring of the Hebrew word שבע *sa'vey'a* – same spelling, with a change of vowels -- which means Sated, as in Satiated, as in Fullness, as in Satisfied, or Complete.[153] As in: "And you shall eat and *sava'ta* שבעת -- be satisfied."[154] The relationship between Seven and Fullness is clearly marked at the very onset of the Torah narrative in her account of Genesis, where Creation achieves completion only after **Seven** phases of becoming.[155] It is **then** that Creator declares "Enough"[156] -- implying a sense of completion, of satisfaction – at least for the time being -- as

---

[145] Genesis 29:20
[146] Genesis 33:3
[147] First Kings 6:38
[148] Exodus 25:37
[149] *Mishnah, Sukah* 4:5
[150] Leviticus 23:24
[151] *Sefer Yetzirah* 4:4
[152] Genesis 41:1-5
[153] 16th-century Rabbi Yehudah Loew of Prague [MaHaRaL] in *Derech Chayyim*, Chapter 5, folio 274
[154] Deuteronomy 8:10
[155] Genesis 2:2
[156] *Talmud Bav'li, Chagigah* 12a

in: "And *Elo'heem* looked at all that it had made, and behold it was all very good."[157] In fact, as the Zohar points out,[158] seven times does the Torah's Creation story recount the will of Creator becoming **manifest** ("ויהי כן And it was so") in Genesis, Chapter One: verses 3 ויהי אור, 7 ויהי כן, 9 ויהי כן, 11 ויהי כן, 15 ויהי כן, 24 ויהי כן, and 30 ויהי כן).

Seven is then more than a number; it represents Completeness, and as such it also implies multiplicity, as in a large number,[159] so that the term "Seven Days of Creation" can just as easily imply **billions** of **years**, as maintained by Rabbi Yitzchak of Acco, who, in the thirteenth century, estimated the age of our Earth to be more than fifteen billion years!![160]

In fact, the Hebraic celebration of the advent of Summer is a single-day festival which, in the Torah, is described as a celebration of the blossoming of the first fruits of the Earth,[161] but which the Jewish people have always known as the Festival of שבועות *Shavu'ot*, literally: "Sevens."

Shavu'ot is indeed a festival of Sevens, during which we acknowledge all the ways in which we are שבע *sa'vey'a* -- full, complete, sated. It isn't that there's not much more than what already makes us happy; it is more about celebrating what is in the moment, as opposed to overlooking it in anticipation of yet more to come. For example: imagine that a delicious-looking red apple sits in your fruit basket on the table before you. It looks just fine. Perfect. Ripe. Complete. But you wonder whether perhaps it could get just a tad **more** ripe, a bit **more** red, **more** perfect…. So you wait. A day, two days, maybe three or four go by, and lo and behold its color darkens to a deeper red. But as you now bite into it, it has become soft, grainy, starchy, and has lost its crisp, juicy flavor and texture, because you didn't eat it when it was complete enough; you tarried in anticipation of it becoming more than it was in the moment. You didn't know when to declare "Enough." *Shavu'ot* reminds us to seize

---

[157] Genesis 1:31

[158] *Tikunei Zohar*, folio 104a

[159] MaHaRaL in *Sefer Gevurot Hashem*, Chapter 46, folio 184

[160] *Otzar HaChayyim*, folio 86b-87b

[161] Numbers 28:26

the blessings in our lives as they come to us, and to not dismiss them as insufficient and wait around for perhaps a later model, a better version. The new and improved i-Phone **50** will come one day, but if we wait around for it without partaking of i-Phone 5 or 6, for example, we will be without phones altogether for at least a year.

This is why *Shavu'ot* is also referred to in the Torah as the "Day of the First Fruits,"[162] reminding us to appreciate the **first** gift that comes our way, rather than letting it pass by in the hope that something even **better** will come along. Indeed it may, but the First Fruit gift is sacred in itself, precious in its own right, and could be the most important "corner stone," so to speak, upon which further blessing will become manifest. As King David put it some 3,000 years ago: "The stone which the builders have neglected, ultimately became the primary stone."[163] Or, as the ancient rabbis put it: "Before you implore God for what you need, first thank God for what you have."[164]

It is no wonder, then, that we have this strange custom on *Shavu'ot* of specifically feasting on dairy products, foods derived from **milk**, since milk is the First Gift we experienced when we first arrived on the planet – namely, the milk of our mothers (or in some cases, Similac). Breast milk was all we needed to feel full, to complete our creation, to feel sated and happy. First Gift alone sufficed for us. And so, on *Shavu'ot*, which reminds us to celebrate **Sevens** in all of the ways in which we have been **Seven'd** in our lives, we feast on milk, on First Gift, on what made us feel full and sated when we first arrived, while we at the same time thank God for the first fruits blossoming in our orchards -- as is.

When we celebrate *Shavu'ot* in this very basic, fundamental way, we are more able to celebrate as well its secondary, accompanying **historical** commemoration, the momentous revelatory experience of the Ten Commandments event at Mount Sinai, the beginning of the **receiving** of the Torah; how we suckled at God's breast, so to speak – Mount

---

[162] Leviticus 23:17 and 20
[163] Psalms 118:22
[164] *Talmud Bav'li, Berachot* 30b

Sinai – to receive the satiating nourishment of Torah as a very potent form of First Gift. As the eleventh-century Rabbi Shlomo Yitzchaki [Rashi] taught: "Just like a suckling child will find fresh flavor each time the child nurses at the breast, so, too, will one who pores over the teachings of the Torah."[165]

The 3,000 who then went on to construct the Golden Calf shortly after this event represented those of us who were unsatisfied with what we experienced at Sinai, or who were unable to retain the enormity of the miracle, or wanted more and more and more, unable or unwilling to recognize First Gift when they saw it. In essence, they demanded more of God than God had chosen to reveal of itself, akin to relationship partners demanding of one another more than is comfortable for either to reveal of themselves, or to gift of themselves, possibly leading to maltreatment. On *Shavu'ot* we declare "Enough." We step back from the urgency of **More**, and celebrate what **Is**. We look without judgment and measurement at all that we have striven for and all that we have attained, and celebrate their preciousness, cherish the blessing of it all, and herald them as First Gift. After all, *Shavu'ot* is the only festival ordained by the Torah that is essentially one day only, not two, not seven, not eight; but **one**. "And before the **One**, what can you count?"[166] for it is about "Enoughing," being sated with one phase at a time, one blessing, one cycle at a time.

Among the many rituals in Jewish tradition involving "Seven" was and is the practice of leaving the land alone every seventh year, during which we are not to work it, not to own it, and allow whoever wishes, whether animal or human, native or outsider, to come into our fields and eat freely thereof.[167] We refer to this sacred season as שמיטה *Shemitah*, ancient Hebrew for "Detachment." Like we do once every seven **days**, on the Sabbath, once every seven **years** too we release, detach, let go of our sense of dominion over the Earth, of our proprietorship of things, animals, people; of our sense of control over our universe, and are

---

[165] *Rashi* on Ecclesiastes 1:9
[166] *Sefer Yetzirah* 3:7
[167] Leviticus 25:3-7

reminded for an entire year that the Earth does not belong to us, nor does anything on or beyond the Earth, including our very existence. None of it, we re-learn, is in our hands. Nor does it end there. After every **seven** times seven years (49) we celebrate the "Jubilee" year during the fiftieth, or, in its original Hebraic vernacular: יובל *Yo'vel*, which at its root implies the act of carrying something away and replacing it with a fresh set of the same. During this time, in ancient Israel, all land was restored to its originally-designated tribal and individual family allocation, all debts were forgiven, all slaves went free[168] – in other words, the nation underwent total **erasure**, so that everyone might have the opportunity to begin anew from scratch and start all over again, economically and otherwise.

The Hebraic mystery tradition understood the *Shemitah* and *Yo'vel* cycles as ritualized microcosmic dramatizations of the macrocosmic cycles of Sevens through which Creation dies and rebirths, ends and begins anew, and that many worlds existed prior to this one; that God created worlds and destroyed worlds, created worlds and destroyed worlds, until this one happened.[169] According to this tradition, the recurring theme of the Seven Cycles is based not only on the seven cycles of Genesis, but on Seven Cycles of existence – period – and that each of these seven cycles, in turn, lasts a period of seven thousand years.[170] This includes six thousand years of life on Earth, after which the seventh thousandth becomes a Sabbatical, when there is nothing, or at least nothing we can possibly fathom, and, in the words of Isaiah, "In that day, God shall reign alone."[171]

This tradition does not profess to know exactly which cycle we are **currently** in, but insists that we are not in the first cycle, and that there were seven-thousand-year cycles prior to ours, at least one, and that, all told, Adam and Eve were therefore not the first humans, only the first humans in this cycle that we are in now. According to the Jewish calendar reckoning, we are currently toward the end of one of those

---

[168] Leviticus 25:8-17
[169] *Midrash Bereisheet Rabbah* 3:7
[170] *Talmud Bav'li, Sanhedrin* 98a
[171] Isaiah 2:11

seven seven-thousand-year cycles, our year at this writing (2016) being 5,776, which leaves us 224 more years until the end of this cycle that we are in right now.

This doctrine, known as the Wisdom of the *Shemitah*, was taught by many of the Kabbalists (Jewish mystics) throughout Jewish history, yet is sadly known today but to a few. One of the more recent mainstream Jewish teachers to dare reintroduce this long-neglected tradition was the nineteenth-century sage, Rabbi Yisrael Lifschitz. Based on these teachings, he wrote, it is clear that dinosaurs and other unusual, prehistoric creatures whose fossilized remains have been unearthed indeed **did** exist, and that they represent remnants of earlier worlds that flourished during the span of earlier seven-thousand-year cycles. And Adam and Eve were then not the original humans, but rather original only in the sense of the form in which humans became manifested in the seven-thousand-year cycle in which we now live. In other words, humans, in one form or another, existed long before Adam and Eve, long before humans as we now know them.[172] Needless to say, the conflict between the Torah's Creation account and Modern Science fades away in light of these ancient teachings.

This tradition may come across as crazy wisdom to some or wild fantasy to others, but what is important to all is their underlying message, that it is at best arrogant for us to assume we know anything about the workings of this magical world we live in, let alone the vast, endless universe in which our world is barely a visible speck. In the words of the twelfth-century Rabbi Moshe ben Maimon (Maimonides):

> The primary source of confusion in our search for the meaning of the universe as a whole, or even of its parts, is rooted in our mistaken assumption that all of existence is for our sake alone. For, if we examine our universe objectively, we will discover how very small a part of it we really are. The truth is, that all of humankind and all the species of life-forms on our earth are as nothing against the backdrop of vast ever-continuing cosmic existence.[173]

---

[172] *Tiferet Yisrael, Sanhedrin*, Ch. 11
[173] *Mo'reh Ne'vuchim* 3:12

Life and Death is then seen in the context of cycles, seasons, part of an ongoing cosmic pulsation that is very much an infinite journey of birthing, dying, and rebirthing, of doing and un-doing and re-doing, of building, destroying, and replacing, of attachment and **de**tachment; a process of constant, perpetual renewal. In our individual, personal sojourn amid this process, we attach and become attached to things, to pets, to ideas, to other people. And, we also, at some point in our lives, are challenged to detach, to let go, to release ourselves from those attachments either through the passing of someone close to us, or by way of our own passing. The rites of the Sabbath, and of the *Shemitah* year, and of the *Yo'vel* year, were intended as one more practice in the here-and-now to prepare for the yet-to-come; one more practice in the realm of the known **Now** to prepare for the unknown **Next**; one more practice in the arena of what we call Life to prepare for the transition through the doorway of what we call Death. After all, Life and Death are but a small part of a series of cosmic seasons and cycles. It is no wonder, then, that the tractate of the Talmud dealing with the wisdom and rituals around death and dying is called: **מועד קטן** – *Mo'eyd Katan*, literally: "The Little Season." For against the backdrop of the bigger picture, it is actually quite small.

CHAPTER SIX

The Ebbing Tide

> Illness separates one from the **collective** self, from the communal or environmental definition of self, and restores one to their unique individual selfhood.[174]

Illness is the opening of the passageway to the other side. It is thus a warning sign of possible death. If it was not the time yet, the medicinal remedies would take effect, and if it **was** time, the most potent of medicinal treatments by the most highly-lauded physicians would be ineffective. We see this in our own time, how sometimes people are healed and sometimes not, and sometimes the best treatment accomplishes nothing for our loved ones and we lose them anyway. Because just as healing is more than medicine, so is illness more than sickness.

Healing is then in the hands of God, or, in the Judaic vernacular: מי שאמר והיה העולם Who-Spoke-and-the-World-Came-into-Being.[175] Therefore, there are times and situations when the least helps the most, and times and situations when the most helps the least. Healing is unpredictable and comes with no guarantees. Sometimes what works for one does not work for another, and vice-versa. This is important for both healer and patient to realize from the onset. There

---

[174] 16th-century Rabbi Yehudah Loew of Prague [MaHaRaL] in *Chidushei Aggadot*, Vol. 2, folio 35 [*Sotah*]

[175] e.g. *Talmud Bav'li, Shabbat* 139a, *Megilah* 13b, *Sotah* 10b, etc. etc.

are circumstances, for example, in which the healing is effective but its efficacy will not manifest until an appointed time, so it may fail today, and three years later suddenly take effect. Because, again, all of it is in the hands of Who-Spoke-and-the-World-Came-into-Being. We can only go through the motions of acting from the place of our finite knowledge and capacity, and the rest is up to the very personalized and customized individual life walk of the individual. This is called השגחה פרטית *hash'gachah pra'teet*, God's personal directing, guiding, supporting, etc. of the individual. We can conjure forth the healing powers of stones, plants, herbs, medicines, pills, spirits, angels, and so on, but the capacity of any of these to actually heal is in the hands of their Creator. Nevertheless, we should not simply seek out just **any** healer but one with proven efficacy and who is deeply learned in and committed to the healing arts. We do not depend on miracles. We do not "test" God.[176]

The Talmud recounts how one of the disciples of Rabbi Akiva (second century) once noticed a man on crutches limping into a house of idolatry, and then, moments later, emerging healed. He asked Akiva how could this be? Do the lifeless idols really have such powers? Akiva replied: "See how great and altruistic is God's compassion. For although this man prayed to wood and stone, nonetheless since it was his time to be healed, God did not withhold his healing. Thus says God: 'Shall I postpone the healing of this one just because his designated time for healing happened to coincide with his foolish visit to the house of idolatry?'"[177]

Among the most important practices around **healing** the sick is **visiting** the sick. It is one of those deeds for which there is no measure, no limit as to how many times one ought to visit the same sick bedridden person. Even if you visited an ill person over a hundred times, you have not satisfied any given measure of the importance of this act.[178] Visiting the sick is deemed so precious that you are rewarded not only in the

---

[176] Deuteronomy 6:16
[177] *Midrash Asseret HaDib'rot*, Chapter 2, end of Paragraph 1
[178] 3rd[h]-century Rabbi Abba Areikha in *Talmud Bavli, Nedarim* 39b

World-that-is-yet-to-Come, but also in **this** lifetime.[179] Visiting the sick is so powerful that it removes from them one-sixtieth of their illness.[180]

> It is written in the Torah: "You should walk in the ways of *Yah* your God."[181] But is it humanly possible to walk in the footsteps of the *Shechinah*? Is it not written that "Yah is a consuming fire?"[182] Rather, it implies the act of following after the *attributes* of the Holy Blessed One, that just as the Holy Blessed One visits the sick, so should you visit the sick, as it is written:[183] "And Yah appeared to him (to Abraham while he was recovering from ritual circumcision) under the sacred oaks of *Mam'rey*."[184]

When you visit the sick, the ancients taught, it is reckoned as if you have resurrected the dead. Once, one of the disciples of Rabbi Akiva fell ill, and none of the sages came to visit him. Then came Rabbi Akiva and visited him. The disciple's spirits were lifted so high from the honor of having the master pay him a personal visit that he declared to Akiva: "My teacher! You have resurrected me!" When the rabbi emerged from the house, he declared to the onlookers: "Anyone who does not visit the sick, it is as if they have shed blood!"[185]

Commenting on this teaching, the early twentieth-century master, Rabbi Yisrael Meir Kagan (*Chofetz Chaim*) wrote: "For it is possible that someone of little or no means does not attract visitors, and this can be fatal since he could be without food or other sustenance required for his illness, and has no access to a physician, nor funds to acquire healing potions. Even more urgent is this during the winter season, for the cold can further aggravate his condition. All of these factors and their like can cause the further deterioration of his condition when, in addition to the illness itself, there exist all of this as well as other such concerns,

---

[179] *Talmud Bavli, Shabbat* 127a

[180] *Talmud Bavli, Baba Metzi'a* 30a

[181] Deuteronomy 13:5

[182] Deuteronomy 4:24

[183] Genesis 18:1

[184] *Talmud Bav'li, Sotah* 14b

[185] *Talmud Bavli, Nedarim* 40a

The Invitation

all of which in the end could **kill** him."¹⁸⁶ These days, if one is unable to visit the sick in-person, one can fulfill the deed by telephone.¹⁸⁷

According to the 12ᵗʰ-century Rabbi Moshe ibn Maimon (Maimonides), even though the injunctions of visiting the sick, consoling the bereaved, and tending to the dead are not specifically spelled-out in the Torah writ and are rather injunctions instituted by the ancient rabbis of postbiblical times, they are nonetheless included in the Torah's instruction to "love your fellow as yourself"¹⁸⁸ -- that anything you would want others to do for you, so ought you to be prepared to do on behalf of others.¹⁸⁹

Visiting the sick also involves running errands for the bedridden as well as keeping clean the room in which they are confined.¹⁹⁰ It also involves empathizing with the suffering of the sick and being moved thereby to pray on their behalf. The ancient sages nonetheless cautioned us that as important as it is to visit the sick and to pray for them from a place of empathy, we should be aware of timing. Often, in the early part of the day, a sick person may not feel as much suffering as later in the day, so it would be better to visit them later in the day when visitation would be more beneficial to them and more tolerable. Toward the **end** of the day, on the other hand, it is possible that the ill person would prefer to **not** have visitors as they grow increasingly tired. The same applies to visiting those whose maladies make socializing more **painful** or stressful than helpful. It is important to not overburden such people with lengthy visitations, or much conversation. Amongst such maladies are severe head-aches, sickness of the digestive system, and of the eyes. When visiting people stricken with these, one should perhaps not even be in the same room as they so as not to intensify the patient's discomfort. Rather, one should remain at the doorway, or in an adjacent area, and only make it **known** to the sick person that they

---

[186] *Ahavat Chessed*, Chapter 3

[187] *Ig'rot Moshe, Yorah De'ah*, Vol. 1, No. 223

[188] Leviticus 19:18

[189] *Mishnah Torah, Hilchot Aveilut*, Chapter 1

[190] 13ᵗʰ-century Rabbi Moshe ben Nachmon [Ramban] in *Torat Ha'Adam*, quoted in Karo's *Shulchan Aruch, Yorah De'ah*, No. 335

are visiting, thinking of them, praying for them, empathizing with their suffering, and that they are available for tending to any errands or other needs on their behalf.[191]

When visiting the sick, the ancients taught, "We do not sit at the head of the bed, for the *Shechee'nah* (Divine Presence) dwells there. Nor do we sit at the **foot** of the bed, for the Angel of Death waits **there**."[192] If it becomes apparent that the stricken individual is dying from their illness, they should be visited initially only by relatives and friends. Others may visit from the third day and on.[193]

We do not share disheartening news with a seriously-ill person, lest we thereby further exacerbate their condition. We do not even inform them that a close-of-kin of theirs has died, including someone like a parent for whom they would be obliged to grieve and recite the *kaddish*.[194] In other words, we do our best not to further aggravate the illness by aggravating the person.

Visiting the sick is a responsibility that knows no age. Therefore it is incumbent upon someone wiser and older to visit an ill individual who is younger, and for an adult to visit a minor.[195] And even though it is customary for a disciple to rise in honor of a master when the master enters the room, nonetheless a bedridden disciple is not obligated to rise in the presence of his teacher who comes to visit him.[196]

When visiting the sick in-person, one can pray in any language since the *Shechee'nah* is present, hovering over their head. If not in-person, it is good to pray in the ancient sacred language of Hebrew.[197] There is no need to mention his or her name when praying for someone in their presence, just as Moses did not mention his sister Miriam's name when he prayed for her healing in her presence: "אנא אל נא – *ana el*

---

[191] *Talmud Bavli, Nedarim* 40a; Maimonides' *Mishnah Torah, Hilchot Avey'lut*, No. 5; Karo's *Shulchan Aruch, Yorah De'ah*, No. 335:8
[192] *Talmud Bavli, Shabbat* 12b
[193] *Talmud Bavli, Nedarim* 40a
[194] Karo's *Shulchan Aruch, Yorah De'ah*, No. 337; *Beit Hillel* on Ibid.
[195] *Talmud Bavli, Nedarim* 39b
[196] *Talmud Bavli, Mo'ed Katan* 27b
[197] Karo's *Shulchan Aruch, Yorah De'ah* 335:5

na -- I [ask that you] please heal her, please."[198] When praying for the sick **not** in their presence, however, one needs to mention their name and the name of their mother.[199] Mentioning the name of one's mother is important in that it is Mother who is the corporeal agent for gifting us with our earthly life force. When praying for one's parent or teacher, however, one does not need to mention their name and can simply say "my mother" or "my father" or "my teacher."[200]

We visit the sick on the Sabbath, but instead of wishing them the customary רפואה שלימה *refu'ah sh'ley'mah* -- "complete healing" – we remind them that "It is the Sabbath, a time to absent oneself of agony; and to know that *ha'refu'ah ke'rovah la'vo'* -- "healing is close at hand and on its way." [201] In Jewish tradition, the Sabbath represents the climax, the completion, of Genesis, of all that was created.[202] To wish someone a "complete healing" during the Sabbath, a period representative of completion, would smack of locking-in and solidifying a particular, explicit and definitive form of what the healing in question ought to look like. Rather, one would instead say "healing is close by and on its way," thus leaving the extent and quality of the healing wide open for further possibility of the form in which the person's "complete healing" might manifest. To wish someone "complete healing" on any other day of the week than the Sabbath is therefore appropriate since all the other days of the week represent the "days" of Genesis during which Creation was in mid-**process** of actively unfolding its endless possibilities.

For one who is dangerously ill, we might perform a ritual of changing their name or adding a new name, to draw forth a different dimension of soul augmentation through the rite of naming, which is empowering.[203] Changing one's dwelling location is also at times

---

[198] Numbers 12:13
[199] *Talmud Bav'li, Shabbat*, 66b
[200] *Shiyurei B'rachah*, No. 335, quoting from *Sefer M'aver Ya'avok*
[201] *Talmud Bavli, Shabbat* 12a
[202] Genesis 2:2
[203] 18th-century Rabbi Chayyim Dovid Azulai in *Sefer Avodat HaKodesh*; 16th-century Rabbi Moshe Isserles [RAMA] in *Shulchan Aruch, Yorah De'ah*, end of No. 335

helpful, as are acts of benevolence,[204] as redirecting our focus from Self to Other not only helps Other but also relieves the Self of its chronic immersion in the agony of the illness.

Healing prayers and rituals notwithstanding, it is always important to remember that healing is not about fixing. It is about **restoring**. And sometimes that restoration cannot be of what was before the illness struck, but rather needs to be more a restoration of the person's passion and life walk in alternate modes within the limitations set by the circumstances of their illness. We cannot always restore physical health and well-being, but we can certainly endeavor to restore dignity, joy, and meaningful living even to those well on their way toward dying. This lesson around illness and healing is alluded to in a Talmudic discussion concerning responsibility toward those in trouble.[205] There, the sages invoked the Torah's injunction regarding the return of a lost animal to its owner: "And if you see your fellow's ox or sheep wandering about lost, you shall restore it to its owner."[206]

Tending to the sick is therefore at core a practice of seeking what it is that might bring them restoration. It is an opportunity for both the individual and the community to restore the preferred dynamics of both the Collective Self and the Individual Self, the dynamics of which often gets confused by the tendency of communal needs to override individual needs. The community is founded upon the assemblage of individuals. If the individuals dissipate, the community crumbles. When an individual is stricken with illness, they withdraw from the collective, and hopefully thereby draws the collective toward them in their time of need and thus restores the balance of the relationship between both.[207] At the same time, illness causes the individual to become more acutely aware of his or her unique self, the Self that exists not **because** of other but in **spite** of other. Here, too, a form of

---

[204] 19th-century Rabbi Meir Leibush [Mal'bum] on Genesis 15:11; *Talmud Bavli, Rosh Hashanah* 16b
[205] *Talmud Bav'li, Sanhedrin* 73a
[206] Deuteronomy 2:21
[207] 16th-century Rabbi Yehudah Loew of Prague [MaHaRaL] in *Chidushei Aggadot*, Vol. 2, folio 35 [*Sotah*]

restoration can take place that will enrich the individual and contribute significantly to the quality of their life if they are healed, or to the quality of their death, if they are not.

A Prayer for Healing
Adapted from Psalm 30, Jeremiah 7:14, Genesis 49:18, Psalms 69:14, and Psalms 19:15

I raise you now in my consciousness, O Infinite One, because I need you to help me open the channels for your healing to infuse this body that you have gifted me. I turn to you now for healing and balance, for it is you who raises my soul from the Abyss, my life force from descending into the pit. I know deep in my heart that the chasm I feel at this time is only for a moment compared to the eternal life-gift that you desire for me. Therefore, while at night I may go to sleep lamenting, I know that in the morning I will awake singing. And often, when things are tranquil for me, I feel like declaring: "Nothing can hurt me, ever!" For I trust in you and await your power to stand me upright and to raise me tall like a mountain of Great Power. Hear me, O Infinite One, and envelop me in your grace; be for me a source of support; overturn for me my grieving into dancing; open wide my capacity to sing in celebration, and let me experience your silence not as absence, but as response.

Heal me, Infinite-All, and enable me to become open to being healed; help me, Infinite-All, and enable me to become open to being helped; because you are behind whatever it is about me that is praiseworthy.

Toward *your* help do I direct my hope, Infinite-All; my hope, Infinite-All, is directed toward *your* help; Infinite-All, toward *your* help is my hope directed.

As for me, my prayer is to you, Infinite-All, during this time of want. Source of all the Powers, in your

magnanimous benevolence, respond to me with support from your attribute of Truth.

May the words of my mouth be congruent with your Will, and may the intentions of my heart be acceptable before you, Infinite-All who is my Rock and my Redeemer.

CHAPTER SEVEN

The Final Moments

> Every person has a star in the heavens that corresponds to them alone. And when they pass from this world, it is only then that their star begins to become visible in the night sky and shines.[208]

When a person is near death, we do not separate from them, so that their soul does not leave them while they are alone and so that they do not die with a sadness over having been abandoned. And it is a sacred deed to be present with one who is dying, to keep them company while their soul is departing their body.[209] It is also special to have at least ten persons present during this time.[210] **Ten** represents the unification of what is diverse, as "10" is actually "1" albeit in its incorporation and uniting of the many.[211] Likewise, death is a homecoming, a process of reunification, of bringing together the many diverse parts of our persona that have played essential roles in the drama of our story. In dying, we are reminded of our essential, unified Self, out of which all of our diverse manifestations of that singular Self originated and within which they are now returning.

---

[208] *Sefer Ma'avar Ya'vok* [Book of "Crossing of the River Ya'vok"], Ch. 30
[209] *Shulchan Aruch, Yorah De'ah* 339:4; RAMA ibid., and *Kol Bo*
[210] *M'avar Ya'vok*
[211] 16th-century Rabbi Judah Loew [Mahara] in *Derech Chayyim*, Ch. 5

If you are keeping a dying person company and there is no one else to replace you who would know how to conduct themselves properly in the presence of a dying person, you may not leave their side even for prayer.[212] Of course, this is common sense, but some well-meaning religious devotees might presume that worshiping God takes priority over comforting one of God's Creations. Needless to say, if something compelling comes up, the attendant should not override their own needs in the moment either, and then feel guilty about it. Each of us is precious, and so are our needs, and no one's blood is any richer than another's.

Those assembled at the bedside of a dying person should not engage in trivial talk[213] but rather speak of sacred matters so that – whether the dying person is conscious or not – their soul will leave in the spirit and atmosphere of the sacred.[214] Care should therefore be taken to ensure that the dying person has complete peace and quiet so that their soul can leave with ease when the time comes. There is also the danger that while departing the body, the soul could be disturbed by sudden noises and therefore return to the body, creating undue suffering for the person.[215] In fact, there is a rule that if a person is dying and there is noise outside, such as wood cutting, etc., that the wood cutter is ordered to cease from his or her work in case the soul is having trouble parting from the body due to the distracting noise.[216]

In certain situations, therefore, even life-support machines can be considered obstructive to the soul's departure. There are times when a person is clinically deemed near death. In such instances, if we see that the patient is in severe agony and that keeping them on life-support will only prolong the agony of their dying, we need to consider their dignity, and the wisdom of forcing them to remain clinically alive while suffering, as opposed to allowing them as peaceful and as painless and as comfortable a death as possible. There are numerous opinions and

---

[212] *Aruch HaShulchan, Yorah De'ah*, No. 341
[213] *Choch'mat Ahdam*, No. 151; *M'avar Ya'vok*
[214] *Sefer Chassidim*, No. 448
[215] *Sefer Chassidim*, No. 234
[216] *Sefer Chassidim*, No. 723

debates amongst Jewish religious authorities around this issue. Ancient Jewish law does not permit actively expediting someone's death, but does permit the removal of factors that are keeping the suffering person alive.[217] In the early part of the twentieth century, Rabbi Naftali Trop, then leader of the ultra-Orthodox Yeshiva of Radun, was suffering intensely while dying. His colleague, Head-Rabbi Moshe Lundinski, immediately ordered his disciples to cease their prayers in case their praying against his death was keeping him alive. Then, sensing that the physicians in attendance were only prolonging Rabbi Naftali's suffering with their treatments, he admonished them as well: "Allow him to die!" he shouted. "Why are you tormenting him? Allow him to die!"[218]

The person who is dying, whose soul is ebbing from its home in the body, is draped in a טלית *tallit* (ritual prayer shawl). The bystanders help him to wash his hands ritually, three times over the right, three times over the left. The dying person then does a little Yom-Kippur-like ritual (if he is able, of course), either verbally or in his thoughts, reflecting on his life, on his past actions and choices, and asking for forgiveness from those he may have wronged.

As he feels himself at the door of death, he recites Psalms 4, 6, 22, 29, 121, and 145.[219] The dying person then declares:

> **I acknowledge before Infinite One, Source of our Powers and the Power of our Ancestors, God of all gods, master of all masters, in the heavens above and in the earth below -- there is no other -- who creates sky and earth, who acts benevolently and justly in the earth, the one who was and is and will be -- that my healing is in your hands, and my death is in your hands. May it be also the will that emanates from before you that I be healed with a complete healing, for you are God of Compassionate Healing. And if I am to die, may my death atone for all of my wrongdoings, whether deliberate, spiteful, reckless, or unintentional. And I further acknowledge and**

---

[217] *Talmud Bav'li, Avodah Zarah* 18a
[218] *Bish'vi'lay Ra'din*, pp. 254-254
[219] 13th-century Rabbi Moshe ibn Nachmon, quoted in *Choch'mat Ahdam*, No. 151; *M'avar Ya'avok*

> believe that God, Creator, whose name is the source from which all blessing emanates, is Creator of all the universes, and alone did emanate, create, form and manifest all, and alone oversees all of the universes, and there is no existence to any of the universes without God's supervision.

When the moment of death approaches, the dying person, if they are able, lifts their fingers upward toward the skies and declares:

> Creator of the universe. I hereby actively and with integrity accept upon myself Death, and I do so with joy and with whole-heartedness, to fulfill the *mitzvah* (sacred instruction) that incorporates all *mitzvot* by joining myself with you and becoming one with your sacred Name. Bring me into the mystery of the Feminine Waters (מיין נוקבין *mayyin nuk'vin*), so that I might by my death unify the Sacred Wellspring with the *Shechinah* in awe and in love, and draw forth from Above to Below, level by level, from your Flux, so that my rising from earth to heaven be a bonding between creation with creator. May my respite be in peacefulness. *Sh'ma yisro'el, ah'do'nie elo'hey'nu ah'do'nie e'chad* – Listen, O Israel, Infinite Mover of All is our Source of Power; Infinite Mover of All renders singular what is many![220]

If the dying person does not have as much time as it would take to recite these last rites, they can of course shorten them, and if they are unable to speak altogether, they can simply **think** the gist of these prayers in their heart,[221] as is written: "Speak them in your hearts, upon your beds, and be thus in the Silence."[222]

While it is important for the dying person to be surrounded during this time by close of kin, such as spouse, children, relationship partners, etc., those present need to do what they can to refrain from weeping in front of the dying person as this would further aggravate the hardship

---

[220] 13th-century Rabbi Moshe ibn Nachmon, quoted in *Choch'mat Ahdam*, No. 151
[221] *Shulchan Aruch, Yorah De'ah* 338
[222] Psalms 4:5

for the dying person.²²³ We must never close the eyes of the dying, for that is akin to extinguishing the remaining spark of their life, and possibly causing their soul to depart before she is ready.²²⁴ The eyes are the windows of the soul, and if the soul sees that we are pulling down the curtains over her, she will presume it is time. Likewise, do we not perform any acts of eulogy or tearing of garments or grieving, or anything else that hints at death itself, such as bringing a casket into the room of the dying person.²²⁵

There is an ancient oral tradition involving the anointment of the dying, while guiding them in thanking their vital organs of their body and bidding farewell to the physical vehicle of their soul. We have composed an expression of this tradition to help those who are tending to the dying:

> **1. Have some fresh, 100% pure virgin olive oil from a bottle never been used before, fresh off the shelf.**
>
> **2. Have a copper basin or other vessel of copper.**
>
> **3. Have a feather. If possible, that of a buzzard you may have found or been gifted. The buzzard carries Life Force that it has retrieved from dying animals. This Life Force was ritually used by our father Abraham in his shamanic vision of the Covenant of "Between the Parts," where he used the Life Force of the buzzard to restore the animals he had cut in half.²²⁶ The soul of the departing is preparing here to be restored to where it had been separated from during its sojourn in this lifetime. Other feathers can be used, of course, the next preferable one being of a dove, which represents future gift, future hope, future life, as the dove was the bird who informed Noah that the Great Flood was subsiding and the earth was being renewed.²²⁷**

---

[223] *Talmud Bavli, Nedarim* 40; *Shulchan Aruch, Yorah De'ah* 335:8
[224] *Talmud Bavli, Eyvel Rabati* 1:4
[225] *Talmud Bavli, Eyvel Rabati* 1:5
[226] 19th-century Rabbi Meir Leibush [Mal'bum] on Genesis 15:11
[227] Genesis 8:11

4. Pour the oil into the copper vessel.

5. Dip the feather into the oil, and begin anointing the person from head to toe, as follows (of course you can use your own words, this is just a guide, so feel free to be creative about it):

Touching the forehead: We thank your mind, for its knowledge, its wisdom, its wit, and for how it carried memories of us and the role we played in your life, how it thought of us always, and remembered our love for you. Thank you.

Touching the ears: We thank your ears for how it served you all the years of your life, bringing to you the sweetness of music, song, voices of those you loved, and learning that helped you in your life journey.

Touching the eyes: We thank your eyes for seeing us in such a good light and beaming at us with so much love, for seeing who we really are, judging us favorably, seeing the beauty of our earth, seeing past all the struggles and challenges you faced.

Touching the lips: We thank these lips for speaking words to us that communicated your love, your caring, your poetry, and that carried forth your voice that was always so soothing and familiar to us.

Touching the arms: We thank your arms for carrying so much for others, for yourself, reaching out to welcome us, to embrace us, to comfort us.

Touching the hands: We thank your hands for giving you so much pleasure through touch all the years of your beautiful life, and for the warmth and love of your touch, and for all that they wrote, built, painted.

Touching the heart: We thank your heart for carrying your life force so diligently and relentlessly through your being all

The Invitation

these years, sending the message of God's will for you to live to every pore of your body, for carrying us in its chambers so lovingly, for feeling so much and sharing so much of what you felt.

Touching the legs: We thank your legs and feet for carrying you all these many years, bringing you to places of beauty, to people you loved.

Following the anointing rite, it may be helpful to whisper delicately to the soul of the dying person:

> Close your eyelids.
> The curtain that veils
> you from the world of
> illusion. For behind
> this curtain there is
> no one and nothing
> Only your precious
> unique self. And
> God Who breathes
> through you.
> Feel this breath.
> Experience the
> Presence. You are
> held. Rest. Lean
> back.
> Surrender into the
> warm embrace of the
> One who is the Only
>
> As you inhale, God
> exhales. As you
> exhale, God inhales.
> God is breathing
> into you. Inhale the
> breath. Now breathe
> into God. Exhale.

Now inhale God breathing Breath into you. Now exhale you breathing Breath into God. Together. You and God alone; Creation and Creator breathing together; exchanging Life Force.

Pay Attention to the Lights. The lights flickering behind the curtain. Behind your eyeballs. Remember these lights. They are the lights of Primeval Creation. They brought you here. They accompanied you on your journey They have been with you always. Remnants of an ancient memory; a memory now waiting to be restored. Gaze upon these lights, the primordial lights of Creation. They are the mysteries that comprise you. They are the forces that are you. They escort you now as you ready yourself to make the transition once more.

**Follow the lights.
They will take you
home.**

**Inhale God's exhale
Exhale God's inhale
When it is time.
When it is time.
The breath you send
back will remain
with God. As will
you. Journey in
Peacefulness. Arrive
in Wholeness.**

CHAPTER EIGHT

When the Soul Leaves the Body

> Seven days after one has died, the soul makes its way to the Cave of *Mach'peyla*. For therein lies the portal to the pathways of the Cherubim, who then welcome the soul and allow its entry into the Garden of Eden.[228]

When the soul has left the body, we shut the eyelids of the deceased, so that by veiling the physical eyes from this world, we enable the unveiling of the soul's eyes to the spirit world.[229] Preferably, we ask the surviving children, if any, to do this.[230] We derive this tradition from God assuring the Hebrew ancestor Jacob that his son "Joseph will sweep his hands across your eyes,"[231] implying a promise that Jacob will not die before seeing his Joseph alive and that Joseph will be the one to close his eyelids upon his death. After closing the eyes, we then sprinkle some earth on the eyelids.[232] We also shut the mouth if it is open.[233] It is important, however, to not shut the eyelids **while** the person is dying, as mentioned earlier, only after it is certain that they have died.[234]

---

[228] Zohar, Vol. 1, folio 219a
[229] *Talmud Bavli*, *Shabbat* 151b; *M'avar Ya'vok*
[230] *M'avar Ya'vok*
[231] Genesis 46:9
[232] *Ma'avar Ya'vok*, *Siftei Ranenot*, ch. 9, folio105a
[233] *Talmud Bavli*, *Shabbat* 151a
[234] Maimonides' *Mishnah Torah, Hil'chot Aveilut*; *Shulchan Aruch, Yorah De'ah* 339

When it is certain that the person has died, we immediately cover their face with pure white linen as a sign of respect and to honor the person's dignity,[235] and we immediately place the body upon the bare earth to protect the departing soul from malevolent spirits that might be hovering about (see next chapter for more about "Bad" Spirits). As we do this, we recite aloud the following:[236]

אדון עולם אשר מלך
Master of the Universe who reigned
בטרם כל יציר נברא   before all of
Creation was formed;
לעת נעשה בחפצו כל   when the time
was that all of his will was done,
אזי מלך שמו נקרא   it was then that
"Counsel" was his name called.
ואחרי ככלות הכל
And after the ending of all things
לבדו ימלוך נורא   shall the Awesome
One reign alone;
והוא היה והוא הוה   and he was
and he is
והוא יהיה בתפארה   and he will be
always, in Beauty.
והוא אחד ואין שני
And he is singular, and there is no second
להמשיל לו להחבירה   to rule over
him, to be equal with him;
בלי ראשית בלי תכלית   without
beginning, without end,
ולו העז והמשרה   and unto him is
the strength and the power.
והוא אלי וחי גואלי

---

[235] *M'avar Ya'vok*
[236] *Siddur* of *Ya'akov Emden*; *Gesher Ha'Chayyim*

Miriam Maron, BSN, RN, MA, PhD and Gershon Winkler, PhD

And he is my God, and my Living Redeemer
וצור חבלי בעת צרה and the Rock of my burdens in time of travail;
והוא נסי ומנוס לי and he is my miracle, and performs wonders for me
מנת כוסי ביום אקרא replenishing my cup in the day that I call.
בידו אפקיד רוחי
Into his hand I trust my spirit
בעת אישן ואעירה in the time when I sleep and when I awake;
ועם רוחי גויתי and with my every breath, even my final breath,
יי לי ולא אירא
God is with me, and I will not fear.

שמע ישראל יי אלהינו יי אחד
Sh'ma yis'ra'el a'do'nai elo'hay'nu, a'do'nai echad
Listen, O God-Wrestler! Infinite Mover of the Universe is the Source of our Powers;
Infinite Mover of the Universe is Only!

ברוך שם כבוד מלכותו לעולם ועד
Ba'ruch shem kevo'd mahl'chu'to' l'o'lam va'ehd (3X)
Blessing Source is the Name, the glory of whose reign is forever and ever!

יי הוא האלהים
A'do'nai hu ha'elo'heem (7X)
Infinite Mover of the Universe is the Source of all Powers!

יי מלך יי מלך יי ימלוך לעולם ועד
A'do'nai meh'lehch, a'do'nai mah'lahch, a'do'nai yeem'lo'ch l'o'lam va'ehd

The Invitation

God reigns, God has reigned, God will always reign forever and ever

The body is placed on the earth immediately upon verification that the individual has passed on[237] because the earth has the power to repel bad spirits and prevent them from impeding the ascending soul. While the body is on the earth,[238] we recite the following, three times:[239]

בית יעקב לכו ונלכה באור יי
אלהים דבר ויקרא ארץ ממזח שמש עד מבואו
יבא שלום ינוחו על משכבותם
הולך נכוח כי עפר אתה ואל עפר תשוב

"Go forth, and let us walk together in the Light of God.[240] *Elo'heem* **calls forth the earth from the rising of the sun to its place of setting.[241] May peace come to those who rest in their places of sleep. Go, then, now,[242] for you are earth and onto earth you now return"[243]**

If the death occurs not in easy access to bare earth, it is good to have some straw or other growth of the earth available upon which to place the body.[244] A fire is lit as well, as fire, too, is believed to drive away "bad" spirits, so if nothing earthy is available, then lighting a fire would work as well. Some traditions have it that the fire is lit even shortly **prior** to the actual death so as to clear the way for smooth departure of soul from body without the impeding presence of malevolent spirits.[245]

The deceased is then returned to a bed, and the following is recited:

---

[237] *Sif'tei Kohen* on *Shulchan Aruch, Yorah De'ah* 339:4
[238] *Sefer Hassidim*, No. 1163
[239] *M'avar Ya'vok; Siddur Rebbe Ya'akov Emden*
[240] Isaiah 2:5
[241] Psalms 50:1
[242] Isaiah 57:2
[243] Genesis 3:19
[244] *Siddur Rebbe Ya'akov Emden*
[245] *Mishmeret Shalom; M'avar Ya'vok, Chey'lek S'fat Emet*, Chapter 15

> Master of the Universe, have compassion upon so-and-so son of/daughter of so-and-so, who has died, and cause his/her soul to rest with the righteous, for you are the one who restores the dead to life, and the living to death; Source of Blessing are you who forgives and relieves us from wrongdoings. And so may it be your will, Infinite One, Source of our Powers and the Power of our Ancestors that you engulf this departed one with angels of compassion, for he/she is a servant child of your maidservant. Therefore save this soul from trauma in its transition, protect this soul from all harm and difficulty for you are the source of all blessing, abundant in mercy and master of compassion, who makes peace and harmony in the beyond for all of your servants and for those who are aware of your essence. And please guide this departed one in the footsteps of the righteous who now stroll in the Garden of Eden, for it is a smooth place guarded by the walking of the righteous. Source of Blessing are you, who gives forth abundant compassion and much consolation to the dead. *Ah'mayn*, so may it be!

Some traditions are against kissing the dead, and discourage close of kin from doing so,[246] while others restrict the proscription to parents kissing their dead children, but that kissing other deceased persons is permissible,[247] as is written about Joseph's reaction to the death of his father Jacob: "And he wept over him and kissed him."[248] The reason for the greater concern around a parent kissing their child is because of the temptation in the moment for the grieving parent to want to follow their child across the threshold of the Land of the Living. Nevertheless, parents should never feel badly about doing so, as often it is difficult to refrain in moments of severe grief. These teachings, it must be remembered, are guidelines, suggestions, to help us along the road to healing and recovery. For example, we are taught to avoid excessive grieving, yet our ancestral patriarch, Jacob, made it known that in no

---

[246] *Bait Lechem Yehudah* on *Shulchan Aruch, Yorah De'ah* 339
[247] *Pit'chey T'shuvah* on *Shulchan Aruch, Yorah De'ah* 394
[248] Genesis 50:1

uncertain terms would he ever cease mourning over the loss of Joseph when he presumed him dead.[249]

Following the departure of the soul, the windows of the room in which the deceased lays are opened as well, to allow for the soul to make its exit with ease.[250] One may wonder why this is necessary, as souls are purely spirit and would then be able to pass through physical "impediments" such as walls. The key to understanding this practice lies in the wording: "to make its exit with **ease**." Since immediately at death the soul is still in "body mode," not having completed its transition, it may be yet unaware of its capacity to overcome physical barriers, and we want to make its journey as easy as possible.

Another practice is the covering of any mirrors in the room where the departure has occurred. This practice, too, is probably related to the "ease" with which we are trying to accommodate the soul in her departure. Again, not yet accustomed to being out of her physical embodiment, the soul may be horrified by the absence of its image in the mirror's reflection. There is even a tradition that calls for covering **pictures** of people,[251] to avoid distraction to the departing soul. And any water lying about uncovered is thrown out the front door into the public thoroughfare as a way of announcing that someone has died, rather than verbalizing the news. Therefore, we do not perform this rite on the Sabbath so that we do not bring sadness to the community on the Sabbath.[252] The waters are poured out also because it is believed that the Angel of Death leaves drops of the Blood of Death in the water.[253] The oldest allusion to this custom is to be found in the Torah's account of the death of Miriam the Prophetess, sister of Moses: "And Miriam died there, and they buried her there, and there was no water left for the assembled"[254] -- implying that the people had poured out their water.

---

[249] Genesis 37:35
[250] *Ma'avar Ya'vok, Cheylek Sif'tei Tzadok,* Chapter 26
[251] *Gesher HaChayyim,* Chapter 3
[252] *Tshuvot Shemesh Utz'dakah*
[253] *Chessed shel Emet,* p. 29, No. 26
[254] Numbers 20:1-2

If the water in the dwelling of the deceased was not thrown out, we refrain from drinking from it or eating anything that had come in contact with it.[255] The dwelling space of the deceased, according to some authorities, includes the entire house in which the deceased is laying as well as any two adjacent homes.[256] However, it does not include a hospital situation.[257] We perform this rite also for a suicide.[258]

At the time of death, or of hearing news of the death, close of kin tear their garment at the area over the heart[259] in respect to the fact that the body had been the garment of the soul all these years and the two are now separated, torn, from one another.[260] *K'riah* קריעה, as this rite is called in Hebrew, symbolizes ripping off the physical garment of the soul to help the departed soul free itself from its physical embodiment.[261] Thus the ancient rabbis instructed that the garment tearing rite be performed immediately upon the departure of the soul from the body, to mark that separation.[262]

When tearing one's garment for the death of one's parent, one must do so with one's hands. For other close of kin, one may use an instrument such as a knife or scissors.[263] When grieving over a deceased parent, the mourner may not repair the torn garment for the first thirty days, not even with a different colored thread, but for other relations one may sew the tear after seven days with different colored thread, and with normal repair after thirty days.[264] After the seven days of grieving, the mourners should not continue wearing the clothing that was torn during this rite.[265] They should either mend the garments or wear something else so that the healing might begin, unimpeded by

---

[255] Rabbi Akiva Eiger quoting the responsum of *Bait Yehudah*
[256] *Pit'chey T'shuvah* on *Shulchan Aruch, Yorah De'ah*, No. 339
[257] *Kol Bo*
[258] *Chessed shel Emet*, p. 30, No. 33
[259] *Shulchan Aruch, Yorah De'ah* 340:2
[260] Responsa of *B'er Moshe*, Vol. 2, No. 117
[261] *Ma'avar Ya'vok, Siftei Ranenot*, ch. 9, folio 105a
[262] *Talmud Bavli, Mo'ed Katan* 25a
[263] *Shulchan Aruch, Yorah De'ah* 340:14
[264] *Talmud Bavli, Mo'ed Katan* 22b
[265] *Chessed shel Emet*, p. 59, No. 24

deliberate visual or sensory reminders of the drama of the death. The **fact** of the death of course remains and is honored with continued mourning rites lasting up to a year, but the **drama** of the passing needs to be allowed to gently and gradually fade-away so that healing and restoration may have their space.

We also perform all of the aforementioned rites of respect and mourning for one who has committed suicide[266] even though suicide is a severe prohibition in Judaism. This is because we cannot render any judgments around why it is that the deceased took their own life, "for no one can know the pain of another."[267] The Talmud brings an example of a young boy in the first century who committed suicide because he feared his father's rage over some wrong he had done. When they asked Rabbi Tar'fon what to do, he replied: "Do not deprive him of one iota of the honors and rites of burial." A second incident recounted concerned a young boy who shattered some pottery on the Sabbath, and fearing his father's terrifying temper, he ran off and committed suicide. They brought the case to Rabbi Akiva, who gave them the same ruling: "Do not deprive him of a single iota of the honors and rites of burial."[268] Such occurrences spurred the second-century sages of Israel to declare that it was strictly forbidden for men to terrorize their families and instill fear in their homes.[269] And they may never **threaten** punishment. Rather, either discipline the child in the very moment of their wrongdoing, or let it go, but never threaten the child with what will or might happen to them. The ideal modality for doling out consequence, they taught, requires us to "distance with the left hand while drawing near with the right hand,"[270] implying the need to show disapproval of the wrong committed while at the same time also demonstrating that love and caring has not been overridden by the disapproval.

Prior to the ritual of tearing their garments, the mourners recite:

---

[266] *Ramban* and *Tur*; *Chatam Sofer* on *Yorah De'ah*, No. 326
[267] *Talmud Bavli*, *Yo'ma* 85b
[268] *Talmud Bavli*, *Eyvel Rabati* 2:4-5
[269] *Talmud Bavli*, *Gitin* 6b-7a
[270] *Talmud Bavli*, *Eyvel Rabati* 2:6

Infinite-All has given, and Infinite-All has taken; may the Name of Infinite-All be for a blessing. Source of Blessing are you, Infinite-All, Source of our Powers, Sovereign of the Universe, the Truthful Judge. The actions of the Rock are always perfect, for all of God's ways are just; a God of faithfulness and without flaw; who acts with complete balance and rightness.[271] **May God usher you forth with your own deeds of rightness and balance, and may the glory of God gather you up. Rest in peace and sleep in peace, until such time as the Consoler shall come with tidings of peace.**[272]

"Source of Blessing are you, Infinite-All, Source of our Powers, Sovereign of the Universe, who has given us life and sustained us and brought us to this moment."[273]

The ripping of the garment rite is performed while standing,[274] derived from the Hebrew scriptural account of King David, who upon hearing the news of the death of his son Absalom, "**rose up** and ripped his garments."[275] These days, the ripping of the garment is customarily done at any time prior to the burial or at the burial site itself, or upon first hearing news of the demise. But the earlier traditions reflect an era when our people were more in tune with the actual moment of the soul leaving the body. However, we do not rip our garments over the dead on the Sabbath or on the sacred festivals.[276] Rather, we wait until the end of the Sabbath or festival.[277]

Some authorities permit the mourner to change clothes for the tearing rite if the clothes they are wearing at the time of the death or news thereof is very precious, or expensive.[278]

---

[271] Deuteronomy 32:4

[272] *Shulchan Aruch, Yorah De'ah* 340

[273] *Talmud Bavli, B'rachot* 59a

[274] *Talmud Bavli, Mo'ed Katan* 20b

[275] Second Samuel 13:31

[276] *Talmud Bavli, Shabbat* 105b

[277] *Talmud Bavli, Mo'ed Katan* 24b

[278] *Bir'kei Yosef; T'shuvat Mahareel; Gil'yon Mahar'sha* on *Yorah De'ah; Chochmat Ahdam, K'lal* 152, No. 2

We make sure none of the deceased's limbs are hanging off the bed and therefore we prop chairs along the sides of the bed if the bed is not wide enough to prevent this. This is derived from the Torah's account of the death of the Hebrew ancestor Jacob: "And he gathered his feet onto the bed and exhaled and was gathered onto his people."[279]

The body is then taken to be washed. The idea of washing the body is not only out of respect to the garment that had clothed and facilitated the soul, but because, as the 12th-century Rabbi Yehudah Ha'Chassid taught: "When we come into this world, we are rinsed with water; likewise should it be that we are rinsed with water when we leave this world."

Those assigned with the ritual of washing the body are encouraged to first immerse them**selves** ritually in a body of living waters (river, lake, pond, ocean, *mikveh*) in preparation for this very sacred task.[280] Minimally, they begin by washing their own hands ritually, pouring water alternately three times on each hand, and then reciting the following prayer:

> **Master of the Universe, have compassion upon so-and-so son of/daughter of so-and-so, who has died, and cause his/her soul to rest with the righteous, for you are the one who restores the dead to life, and the living to death; Source of Blessing are you who forgives and relieves us from wrongdoings. And so may it be your will, Infinite One, Source of our Powers and the Power of our Ancestors that you engulf this departed one with angels of compassion, for he/she is a servant child of your maidservant. Therefore save this soul from trauma in its transition, protect this soul from all harm and difficulty for you are the source of all blessing, abundant in mercy and master of compassion, who makes peace and harmony in the beyond for all of your servants and for those who are aware of your essence. And please guide this departed one in the footsteps of the righteous who now stroll in the Garden of Eden, for it is a smooth place guarded by the walking of**

---

[279] Genesis 49:33; *Midrash Yalko't R'uvey'nee* on Genesis 49:33; *Choch'mat Ahdam*
[280] *Chessed shel Emet*, p. 60, No. 2

> the righteous. Source of Blessing are you, who gives forth abundant compassion and much consolation to the dead. *Ah'mayn*, so may it be!

The body of the deceased is washed first by pouring water over the frontal part; one pours while another scrubs where the water has been poured. The body is then turned on its left side while the right side of the back is washed, then on the right side while the left side is washed. The body is never placed face down out of respect.

After the body has been washed, it is then immersed in a ritual pool, a *mikveh*, after which it is clothed in a pure linen sheet and placed in a purely wooden casket as organic as possible and absent of any artificial treatment or steel, including steel nails. If the deceased had a *tallit*, a prayer shawl, it is placed over them as well.

The use of caskets for burial, wooden or otherwise, is actually a contemporary phenomenon not actually indigenous to the culture of Judaism. It appears from the ancient sources that coffins were originally used only for **transporting** the dead, not for burial itself.[281] The dead were customarily wrapped in simple shrouds of linen and placed directly into the ground, sans coffin. According to rabbinic sources even as late as the sixteenth century, this method of burial was preferred above all other.[282] In fact, some sources report that the ancient way was to leave the body of the deceased suspended above ground in a hammock-like structure, where it remained, exposed to the elements, until the flesh was completely gone,[283] very similar to aboriginal practices such as those of early Native America. Once the flesh was gone, it was only **then** that the bones were placed in wooden or stone caskets and buried in the earth, or in caverns.

The later practice of burying a full corpse in a wooden coffin nevertheless continued the earlier practice of expediting the decomposition of the body, and doing so as organically as possible. Therefore, the casket is not treated with chemicals, such as stained

---

[281] *Talmud Bav'li, Mo'ed Katan* 25a
[282] *Shulchan Aruch, Yorah De'ah* 362:1
[283] *Shulchan Aruch, Yorah De'ah* 363:4

or painted, nor is the lid fastened with nails other than wooden ones. All of it has to be purely organic and biodegradable. Some sages, like Rabbi Yehudah HaNassi (3rd century), instructed his coffin-maker to create a hole at the bottom of his casket,[284] and from there evolved the present-day custom of having a removable board at the bottom of the casket, to be detached at burial. The whole idea of the use of specifically **wooden** caskets is first alluded to in the interpretive teachings of the ancient rabbis in their discussion of the story of Adam and Eve, who are described in Genesis as hiding "inside the tree of the Garden."[285] The Hebrew word for Tree, עץ *etz*, is also the same Hebrew word for Wood. And so, the teachers rendered the narrative accordingly: "And they concealed themselves within the Tree," that is: "within the Wood."[286]

The deceased, from the time of death to the time of burial should never be left unattended. This is in respect to the deceased as well as to guard them against vermin.[287] If there is no concern about the possibility of vermin, then it is still mandatory that someone be present with the deceased in respect for them.[288] However, they may leave the room intermittently, even to tend to unimportant matters, as long as they are present with the body most of the time.[289]

Those who are assigned to watch over the dead, even if they are unrelated to the deceased, are exempt from all of the positive commandments of the Torah for the duration of their shift.[290] If there are two guardians, they could take turns relieving one the other for the purpose of time-oriented prayer such as the *Sh'ma*. Nevertheless, the guardians are not permitted to study **Torah** while on duty, only to recite Psalms.[291] The study of Torah distracts one from attention to the dead, while the reading of Psalms is actually **respectful** to the dead.

---

[284] *Talmud Yerushalmi, Kilayim* 6
[285] Genesis 3:8
[286] *Midrash Bereisheet Rabbah* 19:8
[287] *Talmud Bavli, B'rachot* 18a
[288] RAMA on *Shulchan Aruch, Yorah De'ah* 373:5
[289] *Ig'rot Moshe, Yorah De'ah*, Vol. 1, No. 225
[290] *Talmud Bavli, B'rachot* 18a; *Shulchan Aruch, Yorah De'ah* 341:6
[291] *Sif'tei Kohen* on *Shulchan Aruch, Yorah De'ah*, No. 341

Some authorities ruled that the guardians of the dead may also not eat or drink or smoke or engage in idle talk within the same room where the deceased is laying[292] while others permit eating and drinking in the same room as the deceased and forbid it only for close of kin, relations who are **obligated** to grieve.[293]

Guardians of the dead are permitted to accept payment for their time. Because although it is forbidden to derive benefit from the performance of the deed of tending to the dead, the guardians -- if hired -- are deriving their benefit not directly from the dead but from the relatives of the dead upon whom lies the obligation of watching over the body, to begin with.[294] Even though a *Ko'hayn* is forbidden to be in a place where there is death except for close of kin, he is permitted to be one of the guardians of his dead kin and sit in the same room of the deceased if there is no one else available.[295]

---

[292] *Sif'tei Kohen* on *Shulchan Aruch, Yorah De'ah*, No. 341

[293] *Aruch HaShulchan, Yorah De'ah*, No. 341

[294] Responsa of *Maharam Sheek, Yorah De'ah*, No. 343

[295] *T'rumat HaDeshen* and *Nekudat Yosef* on *Shulchan Aruch, Yorah De'ah*, No. 373

CHAPTER NINE

"Bad" Spirits

> Ah! But God shall redeem my soul from the grasp of the underworld; for He Himself will surely take me.[296]

There is a lot in this material realm of ours that is unseen and often even un-sensed, like electron-microscopic bacteria, ultraviolet rays, sound waves, supersonic and subsonic sounds, various forms of radiation, and so on. It is highly probable that the ancients dubbed their experiences of these unseen entities or energies as "spirits," but it is equally as likely that what they deemed as spirits and what we today image as spirits are very different phenomena. What most of us consider as spirits originates from Hollywood, Fairy Tales, and religion. What the ancients considered רוח רעה *ruach ra'ah*, or evil spirits, are probably closer to what Louis Pasteur discovered under the microscope. Teachings about not leaving water uncovered, washing hands in the morning to remove *ruach ra'ah*, etc. etc., would lead us to believe that, while many took it to mean evil spirits, there were also those who took it to mean pathogens.

While one can easily interpret the term *ruach ra'ah* to imply disease-causing bacteria, it is not uncommon for mystics to lend a more dramatic, spine-tingling form and definition to otherwise ungraspable concepts. What we often refer to as "spirits" was then understood by the ancient teachers as actual **beings** in the sense that they represent mysterious forces that wield influence in our lives, in imagery and through our

---
[296] Psalms 49:16

senses, whether real or illusory, and for better or for worse. Virtually every indigenous people believes in the existence of such forces, be they perceived as external, such as spirits or demons, or internal, such as our very own Shadow Selves. Which of these is the real deal matters little, only that they be acknowledged as influential to the course of our life processes.

In the Hebrew wisdom tradition, there are basically two sorts of spirits operating in our world: spirits involved in the manifestation of flora and fauna, such as of plants, rocks and animals, even rain, and spirits who flourish just like we do, and have personal lives no less than we mortals. In regards to the first type of spirit, every person, every rock, every blade of grass, every planet or star, has a designated spirit that is spiraling it into existence in every moment. These spirits are in turn being spiraled into existence and empowered by yet other **higher** spirits who are in turn being spiraled into existence by yet other even **higher** ones -- each inhabiting a different spirit realm -- all the way up to the Creator Spirit itself.[297] Each spirit and each spirit world, then, represents a phase in the unfolding of spirit into matter, of the manifestation or fruition of the Creator's intent for Creation to become.

The second type of spirit – often referred to as "Bad Spirit" -- is the שֵׁד *shey'd*, or שֵׁדִים *sheydim* in the plural. Described as half human, half angel, these beings linger in the shadows between the material and the spiritual, capable therefore not only of accessing the energies of either but also of manifesting themselves in the realm of both. In the English vernacular, they have most often been described as "demons," who, in turn, have been blanketly tabooed by many religions, and certainly by Hollywood.

Sheydim may also be the Jewish version of elves and fairies, of gnomes and trolls, and the such; there are good ones and there are bad ones, and they constitute a blend of mortal and spirit, capable of appearing in the flesh at will, or disappearing into thin air at will.[298] They can play tricks on us unassuming mortals, perform supernatural

---

[297] 18th century Rabbi Moshe Chayyim Luzatto in *Derech Hashem* 1:5
[298] *Talmud Bav'li, B'rachot* 43b

feats, even change colors.²⁹⁹ Jewish mystical lore categorizes them into the "night *sheyd*," the "tree *sheyd*" and so on,³⁰⁰ so that it indeed does sound like the lore of fairies and gnomes prevalent in, say, the indigenous cultures of northern Europe. The ancient Greeks, too, had their dryads and naiads, tree spirits, and water spirits.

What *sheydim* really are remains precisely the mystery that constitutes the very core of both their essence and their genesis. In ancient Jewish lore, they are creatures of the Twilight Realm, neither of Day nor of Night, neither completely embodied by the physical nor completely etherealized by the spiritual.³⁰¹ As stateless beings, they are often drawn to statelessness and seek to occupy the unoccupied. The ancient rabbis therefore cautioned against entering a ruin alone because of the possibility that the abandoned abode may be inhabited by *sheydim*: "Because of three reasons we do not enter a ruin alone: because of suspicion [about clandestine immoral activity], because of the danger of falling debris, and because of *sheydim*."³⁰² In other words, they are drawn to the Vacuum, to what was once occupied and is now vacant, to what at one time held Presence and now holds Absence. They could as easily therefore be drawn to a fresh corpse -- the once-occupied embodiment of a soul – as to an abandoned structure. They are drawn to the incomplete, to the un-defined, to what has lost its belongingness, its place, its presence in our world.

> The principle of the matter is that everything created is essentially incomplete. And even if it might appear to you complete and whole, it is nonetheless lacking to some degree by virtue of it not having existed prior to becoming.³⁰³

---

[299] *Talmud Bav'li, Yoma* 75a
[300] *Talmud Bav'li, Shabbat* and *P'sachim* 111a-b; Job 37:11 mentions the rain spirit, "*b'ree*"
[301] *Midrash B'reisheet Rabbah* 7:7
[302] *Talmud Bav'li, Berachot* 3a
[303] 16th-century Rabbi Yeshayahu ben Avraham in *Sefer Ha'Sh'LaH, Toldot Adam, Bet Yisrael* 3:2

The Book of the Zohar, one of the most classical of the Jewish mystical texts, describes the *sheydim* as "half human, half angel."[304] As incomplete manifestations, these beings dance between both the spirit world and the physical world while rooted in neither. These wandering half-mortal-half-spirit creatures are therefore capable at whim of manifesting in temporary material form or remaining invisible altogether: "They eat and drink like mortals, engage in sexual relations like mortals, and die like mortals; they have wings like angels, can foresee the future like angels, and journey from one end of the universe to the other like angels."[305] The dual nature of *sheydim* is a result of their having been created during twilight,[306] referred to in ancient Judaic lingo as בין הערבים *bain ha-arbayyim*, the time "Between the Blendings," or בין השמשות *bain hash'ma'shot*, the time "Between the Suns," a period which is neither day nor night.

> It is not feasible to say that nothing at all was created during [the time] Between the Blendings, for the Settling Time [Sabbath] had not yet arrived. Nor is it feasible to say that something would have been created then as during the previous six cycles of the Creation since [the time] Between the Blendings does not belong to that realm either... Therefore, it appears that entities were created during [the time] Between the Blendings that were not completely natural but yet somewhat *bordering* on the natural.[307]

Conjuring *sheydim* was considered a dangerous undertaking since, unlike spirits or angels, they are not simply divine manifestations of the primordial Light but are just as much manifestations of the primordial Shadow. And just like one wouldn't arbitrarily trust any human, likewise one wouldn't arbitrarily trust just any *sheyd*. The *sheyd* may have its angelic attributes, but it is equally endowed with the less stable and more erratic attributes of the human since it is half angel and half human.

---

[304] *Zohar*, Vol. 3, folio 76

[305] *Talmud Bav'li, Avot D'Rebbe Natan* 37:3

[306] *Mishnah, Avot* 5:6

[307] 16th century Rabbi Yehudah Loew of Prague [Maharal] in *Derech Chayyim*, folio 236

Sheydim exist in between the spiritual and the physical realms. In reality, then, they are not experienced by our senses nor are they confined within the limitations of the physical realm and system.[308]

Sheydim, Demons, Malevolent Spirits – all of these exist in the universe of mystery, in the realm of the unknown. Sometimes we experience what *may* be their presence, sometimes there are inexplicable occurrences that point to their possibility (like a missing sock), but their elusiveness far surpasses our human capacity for discovering them.

In the meantime, it is left to us to do what we can, ritually and otherwise, to keep their influential effect upon us at bay, whether real or imaginary, as outlined in the previous chapter.

---

[308] 18th century Rabbi Moshe Chayyim Luzatto in *Derech Hashem* 1:5

CHAPTER TEN

The Burial

Biological life is basically the process of the element Air drawing from all matter its Fire (warmth) and its Water (moisture), to restore it to the element of Earth. So, as long as we eat, we fuel warmth. As long as we drink, we fuel moisture. And as long as we defecate, we fuel earth -- all of that which Air is constantly drawing from us and from every living being. Thus, when we stop eating and drinking and defecating, the element Air continues nevertheless to draw Water and Fire from us until we become earth.[309]

The Hebrew word for Human is אדם *adahm*, which is a derivative of the Hebraic word for "earth" -- אדמה -- *adahmah*. The human is so named because the human is believed to have been formed out of the Earth.[310] And as for the **soul** of the human, it was fashioned out of the Four Directions, or, in the Hebraic vernacular, ארבע רוחות *ar'ba ru'chot*, literally: Four Winds.[311] Each then returns to where it came from, the body to the Earth and the soul to the Four Winds,

---

[309] 10th-century Rabbi Saadya Gaon in *Emunot V'Dey'ot, T'chiyat HaMeitim*, Chapter 7, folio 222
[310] Genesis 2:7
[311] Ezekiel 37:9

who, in turn, emanate from the single Breath of God that animates all beings. Since we are essentially comprised of both Earth and the Four Directions, the Earth will gladly welcome us back anywhere, regardless of our nationality or place of birth.

> No matter where on Earth a person dies, the soil of that place cannot claim: "This one is not made of my dust," for the human was created from earth that was gathered from all Four Directions. Therefore, wherever it is that a person dies the earth of that very place recognizes the body as familiar and receives it.[312]

Burial in the earth is then not all about decomposition. It is also a ritual that acknowledges the most primal origin of all physical life on Earth, and that in essence all living beings belong to her. You may be meandering about in a body that appears disconnected from the earth, and which in no way resembles her, but – in the words of the Torah -- "You **are** earth, and to earth you shall return."[313] While it is true that – unlike First Human who was created directly out of the earth – you emerged from the womb of your human mother, it is equally as true that – whether you subscribe to Science or Religion, or both -- in tracing the ultimate beginnings of your origin as a living being you will inevitably arrive at the earth as the place of your earliest genesis. Therefore, regardless of one's culture, race, or nationality, you are a child of the earth and she will take you back regardless of geographical location. In fact, in the tradition of one 16th-century mystic, Rabbi Yitzchak Luria, where exactly one ends up being buried may be related to a particular part of the original **earth**-formed human of Genesis that over millennia evolved into your distinct latter-day embodiment!

> Here, then, is the mystery of why some people end up being buried in this land, and some in yet another land. For it is known that First Human was formed out of earth gathered from the four winds of the world. It is also known that all human souls are sparks of the primeval soul of First Human, and likewise our

---

[312] *Midrash Tanchuma, Pikudei*, No. 3 [end]
[313] Genesis 3:19

> bodies are offshoots of the sparks of the primeval body of First Human. Therefore, all human souls correspond to one part of the primordial Adamic body or another, this one from the head, this one from the eye, and so on (*Midrash Tanchuma, Ki'Tissa*, No. 12, and *P'kudei*, No. 3). Thus, some people are made of the primordial thumb of Adam and, in turn, of the particular earth from a particular region of the world from which it was formed. Others are from the primordial ear and **its** particular earth and the specific region of the four winds of the world from which it was formed, and so on. Thus some people end up being buried here, some there, some elsewhere, each person returning to the earth from which, in the primordial sense, they originated.[314]

Your body's very primal connection to the earth notwithstanding, the most pronounced and most vivid integral experience during the span of your physical life is your bond with the animating force within you that is your soul. Without the soul, the body is but a lump of clay, a dormant kernel of possibility. It is understandable that, following death, the tie between soul and body would remain for a while. According to some mystical traditions, the soul is still able to see its body from its spiritual abode even **long** after death,[315] and is capable of experiencing the dignity or dishonor accorded its corpse, which is why there are so many intricate rules regarding the handling and treatment of the body of one who has just died.

> Those who tend to the cleansing of the body need to be cautious not to allow any residue from their own skin to fall upon the dead, and those responsible for preparing the grave and placing the body into the earth should be cautious not to drop any soil on the face of the dead. For the soul is very sensitive to any indignity that befalls the body even after death.[316]

---

[314] 16th-century Rabbi Yitzchak Luria, quoted in *Kit'vei Ha'Ari, Sha'ar Ma'amarei Cha'zal, Sukkah* 53a

[315] *Sefer Chassidim*, No. 1163

[316] *Ma'aver Ya'vok*, Chapter 25 [beginning]

There are various customs regarding the לויה *le'vayah*, the ritual of "escorting" the body as it is carried to the gravesite. These can be found in most any traditional Jewish prayerbook. The most common one is that of chanting Psalm 91 while lowering the casket onto the earth with the recitation of each stanza. The casket is carried a few steps, placed on the earth, carried a few steps further, placed on the earth, a series of seven times, until the procession arrives at the gravesite. This is done, again, for purposes of repelling any "Bad Spirits" hovering about. As mentioned earlier, any connection with earth serves as a potent antidote for fending-off unwanted entities. This is also why one of the more ancient Jewish funeral rites included the sounding of the ritual ram's horn, or *shofar*, at funerals, to ward off death spirits from harming the living.[317]

A deeper meaning behind placing the casket on the earth seven times prior to burial involves the ritual weaving of the thread of unification, of the intimate bond between Heaven and Earth, Spirit and Matter, Creator and Creation. In the Judaic tradition, there are Seven Heavenly Realms and Seven Earthly Realms, or Underworlds, and each is a portal to the other. Each realm of the Beyond and the Within gifts us with its particular attribute during our life walk in the here-and-now, those gifts being: Aliveness, Possibility, Empowerment, Wisdom, Peacefulness, Nurturance, and Love. As the body of the deceased is carried to its burial site, we stop at these seven "stations," meaning we place the body, or casket, on the earth seven times, each time expressing gratitude for one of the seven gifts that was granted the person in their lifetime by one of the Seven Realms of the Earth.

As the body is lowered into the earth, we recite:

> **Compassionate One, remember now the precious soul of** (name of the deceased) **who returned to the realm from which s/he had originally come to spend time with us in this life. May her/his soul be intertwined with your great spirit, the source of all life, and in the warmth and serenity of your wings. May her/his spirit be joined with the spirits of** [her/his] (for Jewish

---

[317] Zohar, Vol. 2, folio 196b

person: our) **ancestors** (for Jewish person: Sarah and Abraham), **and with the spirits of other great women and men who now dwell in the Bliss of Paradise.**

Source of all Blessing are you, *Yah*, **breath of all life, who created** (name of the deceased) **and graced us with the gift of her/his presence in our lives. You chose to bring her/him into being on our plane, and you chose to call her/him back to your realm, in your own mysterious way. We thank you, Creator of life and death for the time we had with our beloved and ask you to comfort us now for our sense of loss in our lives and for our somber encounter with our own mortality in this moment. Renew in us the faith that -- in your unending love --death is but a journey of the spirit from the finite realm of physical being to the infinite realm of your eternal embrace. For the soul of the human is a spark of the divine. Wellspring of blessing are you,** *Yah*, **breath of all life, who is with us in life and in death.**

אל מלא רחמים שוכן במרומים
המצא מנוחה תחת כנפי השכינה לנשמת
שהלכה לעולמה. בגן עדן תהא מנוחתה
לכן בעל הרחמים יסתירהו בסתר כנפיו לעולמים
ויצרור נשמתו בצרור החיים.
יי הוא נחלתה ותנוח על משכבה לשלום ונאמר אמן
Great Power of Compassion who dwells in the Realms of the High, bring forth true repose beneath the wings of your Presence to the spirit of (name of the deceased) **who has gone off to her/his next world. May her/his respite be in the Garden of Eden. Therefore, may the Master of Compassion conceal her/him in the cover of His wings forever, and may her/his soul be bound up in the binding of Eternal Life. Infinite One is now her/his family. And thus may s/he rest where s/he lies, toward peace. And let us say: Amen**

After the casket is lowered into the earth, the bottom of the casket is slid from underneath so that the body will return to the earth more organically and expediently. All who are gathered, beginning with the closest relatives, initiate the actual burial by casting earth on the casket until the burial is complete. The left hand is then placed on the grave and the following is recited:

> **"God shall guide you always; God will take away your thirst in the parched places of your soul, and give strength to your bones. You shall become like a watered garden, like a spring whose waters do not cease to flow."**[318]

Upon leaving the gravesite, the gathered do not speak to the mourners other than wishes for healing and consolation, as well as any important matters pertaining to their immediate needs. In absence of the Red Cow ceremony, those attending the burial ritually rinse their hands with water. The encounter with Death leaves us fragile, and sends us into the throes of finiteness and limitation. The ritual of water reaffirms our perpetuity, the continuance of our personal life unfolding in the here-and-now and in the yet unknown Beyond. It is symbolic of the intent to leave Death behind and reaffirm Life.

As the water is poured over the hands, we recite: "May death be swallowed-up forever, and may the Mover of all Forces eliminate tears from upon all faces, and all indignity."[319]

---

[318] Isaiah 58:11
[319] Isaiah 25:8

CHAPTER ELEVEN

Those Left Behind

> Then his servants said to him: "What is this that you have done? While your son was still alive and ill you fasted and wept for the child and refused all food or drink. But when you found out he had died, you rose up and ate bread?" Said David: "While the child was still alive, I fasted and wept, hoping that perhaps God would be gracious to me and let the child live. But now that the child is dead, why should I fast? Can I bring him back again? Rather, I shall go to **him**; but he will not return to me."[320]

From the moment that the dying process begins, until the burial itself, close of kin are called "אונן *o'nayn*." These close of kin are sibling (whether maternal or not), spouse, child, and parent. The word אונן is rooted in the word "אנן *onahn*," which at the same time means "delicate," "oppressed," and "feeling wronged." All of which quite accurately describes the emotional nature of anyone who has just lost someone close, or is in the process of watching them die. Sensitive to the emotional fragility of the *o'nayn*, Jewish ritual law basically goes farther than simply exempting the *o'nayn* from religious duties such as prayer and Torah study but outrights proscribes it, urging the *o'nayn* to

---

[320] Second Samuel 12:21-23

instead focus on tending to both the death or pending death and the rawness of their own grief, both of which can easily become neglected by well-meaning religious zeal and a natural desire to avoid facing the tragedy of loss.

Those in the category of *o'nayn* are therefore disqualified from participating as part of a *minyan* for any prayer service.[321] He or she is also strongly discouraged from studying Torah, even on the Sabbath, when grieving rites in general are suspended,[322] nor is an *o'nayn* called up to the Torah for an *aliyah*.[323] The *o'nayn* cannot even respond to the prayers of others with an אמן *ah'mayn*, for example[324] -- and this is because of the honor of the dying and their state of transition prior to burial.[325] The *o'nayn* needs also to be **grieving** during this time, dealing with the death or imminent death of their loved one. Therefore, from the moment the dying begins until the time of burial, the *o'nayn* may not remove their shoes.[326] They are after all on an important journey. The *o'nayn* is also exempt from all *mitzvot*, all "Thou Shalts," but not from the "Thou Shalt Nots."[327]

If the deceased is being shipped to a distant location for burial, such as overseas, close of kin with the status of *o'nayn* must observe the rules of *o'nayn* even if they will not be present at the burial. Rather, they must observe the rules of *o'nayn* until they are informed that the burial has actually occurred.[328]

From the moment of burial, the *o'nayn* shifts to the status of אבל *ah'veyl*, or mourner. And while they are permitted to greet people, wash up, groom, have sex and partake very moderately of wine and meat

---

[321] *RAMA* on *Shulchan Aruch, Yorah De'ah* 341:1; *Mishnah B'rurah, Orah Chayyim* 55:124

[322] *Mishnah B'rurah, Orah Chayyim* 71:7

[323] *Shulchan Aruch, Yorah De'ah* 341:1

[324] *Shulchan Aruch, Yorah De'ah* 341:10

[325] *Talmud Bavli, Aveyl Rabbati*, Ch. 10; *Talmud Yerushalmi, Mo'ed Katan* 16a and *Chagigah* 19b

[326] *Shulchan Aruch, Yorah De'ah* 341:5

[327] *Talmud Bavli, Mo'ed Katan* 23b

[328] *Talmud Bav'li, Mo'ed Katan* 22a; Maimonides' *Mishnah Torah, Hil'chot Aveyl*, No. 5; *Shulchan Aruch, Yorah de'ah* 375:2

while in the status of *o'nayn*,[329] they need to refrain from all of the above when they enter the status of *ah'veyl*, but only for the first seven days of the eleven moons of mourning that now follow.

> Three days are for weeping
> Seven days are for grieving
> Thirty days are for eulogizing
> Eleven months are memorializing
> After that, don't behave as if you
> have more compassion than God.[330]

During the initial seven-day grieving period – known as *shiva*, Hebrew for "seven" -- the mourner is customarily seated upon the earth, or on cushions close to the ground, but of course may sit on a sofa or chair as well if these seating conditions are uncomfortable. The community, friends, neighbors, distant relatives all coordinate together to make sure the mourner is not burdened with food preparations and the such, and arrange for all meals to be served to the mourner without their involvement. Along these lines, visitors to the mourner do not greet them or initiate any form of conversation. Rather, they simply sit beside the mourner and offer silent consolation by way of their presence. They speak only when spoken to by the mourner but refrain from any gesture or verbiage that might interrupt the mourner's grieving or in any way pressure the mourner, subliminally or otherwise, to respond, to step out of their grieving in order to reply. This practice, aside from its reasonable and psychological benefit in consideration of the bereaved, is derived from the Book of Job. In this ancient Hebrew Scripture, Job is grieving a huge loss in his life and is visited by friends and colleagues who attempt to comfort him and to propose possible explanations for his suffering. When they first arrive, however, they simply sit down, remain quiet, and wait for Job to choose when and if to commence a dialogue.[331]

---

[329] Maimonides' *Mishnah Torah, Hil'chot Avey'lut*, beginning
[330] *Talmud Bavli, Mo'ed Katan* 27b
[331] Job 2:13 and 3:1

Upon the conclusion of the visit, whether words were exchanged, or not, the visitor again wishes the mourner healing and consolation and leaves. This particular phase of the eleven-month grieving period lasts seven days, but is suspended on sacred festivals, that is, those festivals mentioned in the Torah: *Rosh Hashanah, Yom Kippur, Sukkot, Sh'mini Atzeret, Passover,* and *Shavuot*.[332]

Mourners do not attend religious services the first Sabbath following the death of close of kin. On the **second** Sabbath, they attend services but do not sit in the customary place where they have always sat. On the third Sabbath, they sit in their customary seating place at the worship service but do not speak to anyone there. On the fourth Sabbath, they return to normal communal conduct.[333] This practice of gradual reintegration into normative living helps the mourners remain in the rhythm of healing as well as of grieving, as both are interdependent. Healing, or "mending" what has been "torn" from the mourner's world, happens in the course of grieving, especially if that process is enabled with the least of interruptions, and with as little of social demands as possible.

There is little difference between the dynamics of a gaping wound in the flesh and a gaping wound in the heart. Both require careful attention, delicate handling, and ample time to mend. Assuring someone that "they'll get over it" only belittles for the mourner the intensity of their pain. Yet, at the same time, the rites of grieving in this tradition are simultaneously intended as well toward gradually and as organically as possible guiding the mourner **out** of their grieving state and back into the continuity of their personal life walk. There is a clear distinction between grief and the possibility of its eventual spill into clinical depression when it is excessively prolonged. In such an instance, it is no longer part of the grieving process as discussed here, but becomes then a serious concern requiring intervention, whether it be pastoral, psychological, or medical.

---

[332] *Shulchan Aruch, Orach Chayyim* 548
[333] *Talmud Bav'li, Aveyl Rabbati*, Ch 10

Miriam Maron, BSN, RN, MA, PhD and Gershon Winkler, PhD

Grieving is not as simple as the act of feeling bad or sad or in pain over the loss of someone close to us. It is far more than this. It is the challenging birth pangs of deep personal rebirth. The loss of someone with whom we were intimately or integrally close is at the same time the loss of a significant chunk of our very own persona that has developed within us and through us and become an integral part of us over the course of our relationship with that someone. Their Death then in turn becomes **our** Death as well, the death of that part of us that was their energetic presence not only in our Life but in our very being. The deeper, underlying reason why the process of grieving is so ritualized in this ancient way is then because, more than the experience of personal loss it is an experience also of personal discovery. In the grieving process, we are challenged to rediscover parts of our unique selfhood that – during our lifetime relationship with the deceased – was veiled, or perhaps even overshadowed by them, or to some degree restricted, or limited, for better, or for worse. In their passing, we are then left with a void, a vacuum within our selfhood that they had filled, that was occupied by their presence in our life, both the agony and the ecstasy of it. In their absence, we are left with a vacant spot in our Gestalt, which the rituals of *avey'lut* -- אבילות --"grieving" gradually empowers us to refill and in which we are enabled to reconstruct where there is now the ruins of what once was, and to re-plant where there now remain but the roots of what once flowered. Ironically, within the grief around the death of Other lies the joy around the birth of Self.

It is no accident that the Talmudic tractate which most deals with the rites of death and mourning is titled **שמחות** *sema'chot*, literally: "Rejoicings." The Judaic mindset does not allow for the total abolition of joy, neither in the place of tragedy nor in the place of grief. It is a mindset founded upon a path that encourages an in-your-face attitude, that is, an attitude of audacity – more popularly known as **חוצפה** *chutzpah* – in the face of anything and everything that would hinder or in any way challenge the gift of Being, the joy and privilege of personally embodying any portion of the Divine Intent, for however long or short a period, and under whatever circumstance.

And so we grieve, and we miss, and we remember, and we long – and we rebuild. And dying becomes part of living. And then, when it is our turn, we are that much more prepared, as are those whom we, too, will one day leave behind.

CHAPTER TWELVE

When Death is Violent

> Only eyes vigilant and fortified against the glaring and superficial can still perceive God's vision in the soul's horror-stricken night of human folly, falsehood, hatred and malice.[334]

What do we do with the seeming paradox of a compassionate Creator of a world where evil runs rampant? How do all of the beautiful teachings of the aforementioned chapters fit in alongside the tragedy of a **violent** death, whether by way of an automobile accident, a plane crash, or a gruesome murder?

To tackle this question, we need to examine some of the givens in the Judaic understanding of God's relationship with Creation, with some of the "fine print" in the meaning of our being here to begin with. We also need to distinguish between the evil that comes about because of human error and misunderstanding, or the evil that just "happens" – like an earthquake, or other disasters commonly labeled "acts of God" – and the evil of deliberately perpetrated atrocities: what we might call "sinister acts."

One of the most fundamental givens of Judaism is that we have Free Will. The ironic part of this is that we do not have Free Will in **regards** to Free Will. In other words, we have no choice but to **have** Free Will. If you will then ask the age-old question whether everything

---
[334] Abraham Joshua Heschel in *Man is Not Alone*, p. 211

The Invitation

is predetermined or whether we have Free Will, the answer would be more like that of the second-century master, Rabbi Akiva: "Everything is predetermined and the choice is yours."[335] In other words, your Free Will is predetermined, but not the choices you make with*in* your predetermined Free Will; you are free to choose, but you are not free to *not* choose.

In this scenario, we are all walking a tightrope, a journey that is possible only by means of constant swaying, constant choosing, between one side and the other. Rabbi Abraham Joshua Heschel put it this way: "If man is not more than human, then he is less than human. Man is but a short critical state between the animal and the spiritual. His state is one of constant wavering, of soaring or descending. Undeviating humanity is nonexistent. The emancipated man is yet to emerge. Man is more than he is to himself. In his reason he may be limited, in his will he may be wicked, yet he stands in a relation to God which he may betray but not sever and which constitutes the essential meaning of his life. He is the knot in which heaven and earth are interlaced."[336]

The Free-Will factor is then both, a blessing and a curse. The blessing is that we have the freedom to make choices that are our very own and that forge our aliveness and rightness in our personal lives and in the lives of those around us. The curse of it is that we also have the freedom and the power to make choices of the kind that *impede* rather than further our own well-being and that of others. Nor is the curse component of Free Will restricted to sinister choices. Ninety-nine percent of illnesses, the ancient rabbis suggested, are due to human recklessness. Ninety-nine percent of deaths, too, they held, are due to human choices and carelessness.[337] Contemporary statistics bear this out as well – though not as dramatically as the Talmud – that, even barring sinister mortal choices of war and home-front assaults, most deaths and illnesses occur due to human recklessness, from drunk or incompetent driving to destructive diets and lifestyles. Not to excuse those making

---

[335] *Mishnah, Avot* 3:15
[336] *Man is Not Alone*, p. 211
[337] *Talmud Bav'li, Ketuvot* 30a; *Midrash Vayikra Rabbah*, Ch. 16; *Talmud Yerushalmi, Shabbat* 43a

decisions that negatively impact others with no good intentions, but, in general, people do not always act from a clear, conscious place, which is what perpetuates this problem, unhealed. And sometimes it is their choice not to choose or get help to heal.

Yet, the tendency is often to blame God for our ills, for either causing them or enabling them. In times of tragedy, we are inclined to ask: "Where is **God**?" – only to then deafen our ears to the question echoing right back at us, the very first question God asked the very first human: "Where are *you*?"[338]

In essence, Good and Evil are both creations of the One God.[339] Both share the same tree,[340] and neither have any existential reality of their own other than that which we accord them by way of the choices we make and the actions we take. For example, God did not create donuts, only wheat and sugar cane. Donuts were created by the choices we made about wheat, about the dormant potentials of life's givens, of life's possibilities. Likewise, God created the capacity for good and evil – their possibility – but it is *we* who make the choices that give form and definition to either one, for better or for worse.

Good and evil, therefore, take on their form by the Free-Will choices of human reasoning and grappling. Good is then not always the better. Evil is not always the worse. It is evil to lie, and it is good to tell the truth. But if telling the truth would endanger an innocent life, is it still *good*? And would lying then still be *evil*? As absolutes they have no footing on this plane. They come alive only in dance, only when activated by the relative nature of human experience. They then become seeds of potential, which bear fruits of one or the other according to the intentions that forge our choices.

Sinister evil aside, there is also the kind of experience that can go either way, depending upon subjective interpretation. A single experience can to one person seem evil, and to another, good. A particular medicine may be poison to one and a sure cure for another.

---

[338] Genesis 3:9
[339] Isaiah 45:7; Proverbs 16:4; Lamentations 3:38
[340] Genesis 2:9

The Invitation

Roses are attractively colored and fragrantly scented, but they are also surrounded by painfully annoying thorns, and some people are terribly allergic to them. In addition, sometimes an experience may seem bad initially but in the end be understood as good. The dentist's drill is painful and a very "bad" experience, yet it is also "good" in that its end purpose is to repair decaying teeth and thereby prevent the development of far more painful consequences.

Opposites, we are taught, are dual phenomena only in relationship to subjective human perception, but to God all opposites are unified[341] and serve a common divine purpose: "For this too opposite the other, did God create."[342] Evil, for example, can compel the good to surface. It can also be harnessed toward good ends. The Judaic concept of Satan is described in this context. The mythic archangel of evil – called השטן *Ha'Satan* in the Hebrew, or "the one who obstructs" – is portrayed as a force of opposition not to God but to humans, assigned the role of proving our soul-deep convictions by challenging the credibility of the "good" of which we boast, or by bringing its latency to the forefront. In the biblical Book of Job, for instance, The Satan brings tragedy to a righteous and innocent Job only after consulting with God and receiving divine license to do so toward the purpose of validating Job's acclaimed piety.[343]

The Talmud recounts an amazing story about a man named Plimo.[344] Plimo was a righteous man who lived in Jerusalem in the first century, B.C.E. He was a wealthy and very successful merchant known for his charitable ways and he was blessed with a beautiful family and a huge, luxurious abode. As part of his daily religious devotion, he would add his own prayers asking God to please keep The Satan away from him and from his family, and then he would proclaim: "An arrow in your eye, O Dark Angel!" And thus he went about satisfied that he'd driven away any impulse toward sinfulness by his daily bold appellations against The Satan.

---

[341] Psalms 139:12
[342] Ecclesiastes 7:14
[343] Job 1:6-12
[344] *Talmud Bav'li, Kidushin* 81a

One Yom Kippur Eve, when Plimo sat comfortably around his dinner table surrounded by his honorable guests and his perfect family, a filthy disheveled vagabond arrived, knocking ferociously on Plimo's door. It is customary on the eve of this holiest day of the year – the Day of Atonement -- to celebrate with a lavish feast as is befitting a festival such as this, to remind us that even though we will be fasting from nightfall to nightfall, it is still a *festive* period, as we rejoice in our faith that God will forgive our sins on that very day.

And so there they were, eating and drinking, Plimo seated proudly at the head of the table all bedecked in his finest and feeling beside himself, in a good way, when this repulsive beggar comes knocking in the middle of this very sacred feast. Plimo, being the benevolent patron that he was, rose immediately from the comfort of his cushions, swung open the door, and brought the stranger a plate of delicacies and some bread, even some wine, and placed it on his front porch for the man to sit and eat there.

No sooner had Plimo sat back down at the table inside the house when he heard the beggar begin to snarl and grumble.

"So!!" the man yelled, "everyone sits on cushions inside the comfort of the house and I have to sit out here on this hard cold stone bench?!"

Plimo rose up, went outside and invited the man inside, and, because of his stench, seated him in a corner a good distance away from the dinner table. No sooner had Plimo rejoined his guests when he heard the beggar begin to snarl and grumble again.

"So!!" the man yelled, this time even louder, and foaming at the mouth, "everyone gets to sit together around the dinner table and I have to sit here in the corner all by myself?!"

Plimo rose up again and escorted the stranger to the table, much to the disappointment of his guests who by now were trying not to inhale too deeply due to the stench of urine and mildew. The man sat down on one of Plimo's favorite cushions, sipped from his goblet, then spat the wine out in disgust. Then he dipped a filthy hand into the shared soup bowl to retrieve a chunk of meat, tasted it, and spat that out too.

Plimo could no longer contain himself. He rose up out of the comfort of his cushions, walked over to the man, seized him by the arm, and began shouting angrily into his mud-covered ears: "How dare you come into my home and insult me, my family, my guests, my mother-in-law's cooking!! I have been more than gener...."

The man, however, shocked by the assault, dropped his plate, and fell to the floor, unresponsive.

Plimo knelt by the man, checked his pulse, ordered a feather be held over his nostrils, and it then dawned upon him like a meteor crashing down upon him from the skies that the stranger was **dead**, that he'd caused a man to **die**!!!!!! -- and on the eve of **Yom Kippur** to **boot**!!! Plimo up and fled, running far from his beautiful home and into the hills. He ran and screamed and wept. He could not believe it!! Here he was preparing to enter the holiest day of the year, the Day of Atonement! And he had lost his temper and **killed** a man!!! His entire life was ruined!! What was there to live for now!? How could he ever again celebrate Yom Ki....

His laments were suddenly interrupted by a gentle tap on his shoulder.

With great trepidation, Plimo turned around.

It was **him**. The beggar. The dead man. Except he wasn't dead, after all. Before Plimo could utter a sound, ask a question, express an emotion, the filthy, smelly, disheveled stranger began to shape-shift before his eyes, and within moments the repulsive stranger morphed into a beautiful, glowing, angelic being.

"But who...who...what...who are you?" Plimo could barely speak.

"I am he, the one you pray against daily, Plimo, the one in whose eyes you keep shooting imaginary arrows; the one you keep asking God to keep away from you and your family."

"You are **he**? The **Satan**? The Angel of **Darkness**?"

"I am he."

'Why did you frighten me like this? You have no idea how terrified and hopeless and horrific and...."

"Horrific, you say? Well, isn't that how you have thought of me all along? Isn't that the theme of your prayers about me? So what did you **expect**?"

"Well, what **should** I pray about you?"

"Pray that God help me to keep doing good in the world."

"You doing *good*? But I thought that you...."

"That I am all about evil. Well, I will have you know that what I did to you tonight was a good thing, a precious gift, for until this moment you would have entered this holy of all days presuming you were righteous and sinless, when all along, festering inside of you, was the potential to blow up at some poor helpless hungry beggar and have him thrown feet first out of your home. Now, however, that dormant sin has been externalized, cut out of you like a boil removed from a diseased person, and you can enter Yom Kippur clean and whole, a truly remorseful penitent who has confessed what he might never have had the opportunity to confess about himself, having for so long veiled it comfortably beneath self-righteousness and in the guise of religious piety. It is my job to call your bluff and put your convictions to the test, and so I have. What I gave you was evil, but what you received was good. And now your Yom Kippur will be the most beautiful and most sacred and most meaningful than ever it was."

And with that, The Satan flapped his wings and flew off into the realms of the Great Unknown. And Plimo lived happily ever after, and never again uttered so much as a single negative word in regard to The Satan, for he had never been so enlightened by anyone as he had by the Angel of Darkness himself.

Then there is the tragic effects of chaos in the world, of earthquakes, volcanic eruptions, genocides, famines, random slayings, ritual abuse, and fatal epidemics; of either humanity or nature gone berserk and slipping backward across the line of Creation into the chaotic abyss of Genesis, the primal cauldron in which life and death churn and ferment in the seething admixture of paradox, and where life and death are easily confused for one another, the boundaries between them blurred and deceiving. It is an unpredictable form of evil, void of any definitive pattern, subject to chance and circumstance, indiscriminately striking both, the righteous and the wicked, the guilty and the innocent alike.³⁴⁵ It brings in its wake a terrifying sense of helplessness and incomprehensible torment. It is the stuff of nightmares experienced by survivors of holocausts, child abuse, rape, and other terrors. It is what makes us call out at times: "Where is the God of justice?!"³⁴⁶ -- and which moved many in times of tragedy to declare: "There is no judge and there is no justice; God has abandoned his world and gone off to sit in the heavens!"³⁴⁷ It is the cry most every one of us has experienced at one time or another when there were no answers, not even imaginary ones, when nothing made sense; when it so blatantly seemed that God was indeed absent, or even completely nonexistent. It is the encounter with the Force that emanates from what the ancient Jewish mystics referred to as the סטרא אחרא *Sitra Ach'ra* – "the Other Side." For when we make our choices and commit our actions far from the clarity of the God-Light – of the God-Will that there be life and joy – we risk crossing the Line of Life and slipping ever so gradually into the Other Side; we risk losing our Selves in the realm of the *Sitra Ach'ra*, where everything is one great undiscernible glob, void of distinction. There, the boundaries that mark life and death, right and wrong, are confused, and our mortal manifestation of soul becomes distorted, mistranslating the cries of our tormented spirits into twisted exhilaration in our now out-of-control embodiments. There, our pleas to desist sound like demands to *p*ersist.

There is indeed that possibility in life, for the human – in fact, any one of us – to fall so far from the God-Light that we would perpetrate brutality, whether in the name of "political correctness" or religious belief, or some other super-rationalized agenda that enflames vindictiveness toward others or ourselves. When we are the victims of such evils, we cry out from where we experience the pain – our bodies, and often our hearts and souls. And when we are the perpetrators we cry out as well – from our souls, which, too, languish in torment.

---

³⁴⁵ *Talmud Bav'li, Baba Kama* 16a
³⁴⁶ Malachi 2:17
³⁴⁷ *Midrash Tehilim* 10:6

> And God said [to Abraham, in response to Abraham's curiosity as to why the angels who had just visited him were heading toward Sodom: "They are being sent there because of] the cries of Sodom and Amorah, for they are excessive, and [in response to] their wrongdoings, for they weigh heavily. Please allow Me to descend and let Me see whether the cries that have come to Me match the degree of destruction they have wrought, and if not, I will know."[348]

Even the sadistic smile of a coldhearted murderer, then, veils the intense sadness of a shattered soul engulfed within the whirlwind of chaos and confusion. This does in no way excuse the evil committed nor the person behind the deed. But the Judaic understanding of evil seeks to penetrate the surface level of its experience to grasp the heart of it; to break through the seemingly impregnable bulwark of this intimidating energy, which often seems more powerful than we, and disassemble it piece by piece; to follow it to its very end in order to discover even there – God:

> In the prophet Ezekiel's vision, he saw "a stormy wind sweeping out of the north, and a great cloud, with brightness all around it, and with fire flashing forth from it continually" (Ezekiel 1:4)….. The "great cloud" represents the force of destruction in the world and it is called "great" because of its darkness which is so intense that it conceals and renders invisible all sources of light, and thus overshadows the entire world. The "fire flashing forth" alludes to the fire of stern judgment that is attached to it. "With brightness all around it" means that although it is in itself the very arena of ultimate defilement, it is nevertheless surrounded by a particular degree of light…. It possesses an aspect of the holy and should therefore not be altogether regarded lightly, but should rather be allotted some degree of space in the arena of holiness.[349]

> When God created the world and wished to reveal that which was concealed within the depths of the Abyss and to disclose the

---

[348] Genesis 18:20-21

[349] Zohar, Vol. 2, folios 203a-b

light from out of the darkness, they were all merged with one another, and therefore did light emerge from darkness, and also did the profound come forth from the mystery. Each came from the other. Thus, from Good can come Evil, and from Mercy can come Judgment. All are intertwined, the good as well as the evil impulse.... For each was at one time interdependent, one upon the other.[350]

There is nothing of the Other Side which does not also have a spark of the Divine Light within it.... All things cleave one to the other, the pure and the impure. There is no purity except through impurity.[351]

It would seem from these teachings that, as the eighteenth-century Rabbi Avraham Azulai wrote, "It is the very spark of holiness present even within evil that enables its existence,"[352] and that without it, evil would be but illusory and powerless and fade into oblivion like a threatening thundercloud looming momentarily before dissipating into nothingness. This concept is certainly an enormous challenge to anyone who has suffered by the evil choices and actions of others: an actual spark of the God-Light even in the most sinister of nightmares? Is God really present and with us even in the moment of a tragic experience, of our being victimized? How can we reconcile the seeming contradiction of a God who would instruct us "not to stand idly by the blood of your fellow"[353] and not to turn away when someone needs help with so much as their donkey,[354] and who yet often seems guilty of both?

Welcome to the Garden of Paradox. Here, there is no light without the accompanying background of darkness, and no good without the possibility of bad to define it. Everything defines its opposite by virtue of its contrast.

---

[350] Zohar, Vol. 3, folio 80b
[351] Zohar, Vol. 2, folios 69a-b
[352] *Or Ha'Chamah*, Vol. 2, folio 218a
[353] Leviticus 19:16
[354] Deuteronomy 22:3-4

> God has also set one thing opposite the other; the Good opposite the Evil, and the Evil opposite the Good; Good from Good, and Evil from Good; the Good defines the Evil and the Evil defines the Good.[355]

While evil and suffering are certainly not necessary prerequisites for existence, it is nevertheless only in a realm of opposites that Free Will can flourish, for where there are opposing options there are also opposing choices. The capacity for opposition is as vital to the human spirit as is oxygen to the human body. It is the psychic and spiritual atmosphere necessary for us to thrive as humans, as conscious beings capable of individual choice.

In a universe endowed with Free Will, it is hardly obvious to us whether a particular tragedy occurs by Divine Directive or is just one of those vague, random events. For example, if we were to run across a busy intersection blindfolded and suddenly find ourselves atop the hood of an oncoming pick-up, random carelessness would be a more educated guess than either Divine Directive of random evil. If, however, we walked cautiously out into that intersection, looking both ways, and suddenly got hit on the head by a meteor, something we could absolutely not control, then we might guess that it was possibly an Act of God, but only possibly, because again, we sojourn in a universe of Free Will. And in order to allow for that Free Will to be, God may not consistently manifest conspicuous Presence or Guidance. Otherwise there would be no room for doubt, and therefore no place for faith; no room for error, and therefore no place for correction; no room for question, and therefore no place for knowledge; no room for failure, and therefore no place for growth. And so, everything God made, "God saw that it was Good,"[356] implying at the same time the emergence of Evil, for the very mention of "Good" implies the very existence of Evil no less than the very mention of "light" implies the very existence of "darkness."

Likewise, Free-Will, too, was created by God, as only it could have, wrote the 16th-century Rabbi Yehudah Loew: "The concept of Free-Will

---

[355] *Sefer Yetzirah* 6:4
[356] Genesis 1:4,10,12,18,21,25, and 31

did not originate in man; it is a creation by God. For example, two men share a boat. Can they grant one another free choice? Not at all. For what if one wishes to sail west and the other east?"[357]

If all were clear-cut, black-and-white – if only the guilty suffered – there would be no choice but to believe in and draw close to God effortlessly, meaninglessly, purposeless, like puppets or robots rather than like humans, by compulsion rather than by choice and conviction. If all were Light, we would be as incapable of seeing as we would if all were Dark. Together, the opposites dance a choreography of isometric push and pull and can only maintain their balance as long as both remain organic and continue to weave up as well as down, right as well as left, forward as well as backward, each step and movement playing out the choices and actions of the Human on Earth under the observation and guidance of the Great Cosmic Dance Instructor who watches from afar but who is yet as "close to you as is your ear to your mouth."[358]

> In the Time to Come, the Holy Blessed One will display the Evil Force before the righteous and the wicked and shall destroy it in front of them. To the righteous, it shall appear as a huge mountain, and to the wicked it shall appear as a single strand of hair. Both the righteous and the wicked shall then weep. The righteous shall weep out of joyous amazement and exclaim: "How did we ever overcome so great a power?" And the wicked shall weep out of intense shame, and exclaim: "How could we have succumbed to such a weak force?"[359]

Therefore, free reign is given erratically to circumstance, as in hurricanes and earthquakes, as in plans that don't work out, as in prayers that aren't answered (at least not in the way we had wished), in order to preserve Free Will in the world and thereby ensure the perpetuation of opportunities for personal growth and ennoblement. But whether by carelessness, an "Act of God," or natural circumstance,

---
[357] Maharal in *Ohr Chadash*, folio 91
[358] *Talmud Yerushalmi, Berachot* 13a
[359] *Talmud Bav'li, Sukkah* 52a

we cannot always know which is which, and must take each pain in life as an opportunity to grow and to improve. If we hurt ourselves through obvious neglect or carelessness, we need to learn to be more careful. Then, not unlike a cardiac patient, we need to reevaluate our lifestyle, the direction we are taking, and attempt to make some appropriate adjustments. We might then consider the experience as an attempt to protect us from an even greater calamity, whether on the physical or spiritual plane of existence, "for whom God loves, does God reprove, as a parent would their child."[360]

If we hurt due to circumstances beyond our control, we might salvage what we can of the lessons that can be extrapolated from the rubble of the experience, although we should certainly not allow the gift of the life lesson to justify the tragedy it brought. We could learn, for example, how Free Will is more than a gift; it is a serious responsibility with weighty consequences, no less than the handling of a loaded pistol. When misused, when exercised from the *Sitra Ach'ra* place, it can empower human beings to damage others, and to thwart the flow of Free Will from other human beings. The imperfections of the material world will at times also remind us of how this world is designed as a means toward a higher end. We are not obliged, however, to take the blame for what happens to us, to always attribute death and suffering to wrongness on our part. "There is death and suffering even without sin," taught the second-century Rabbi Shimon ben El'azar.[361] And if a person who has been the victim of natural disaster or sinister assault is able to somehow reclaim their Free Will piece by piece and to turn the experience around a little or a lot – if that person can heal, can wrestle gifts out of a tragic situation and end up functional, or okay, or even stronger than before – the credit belongs to them, and them alone, not to the disaster and not to the perpetrator. Nevertheless, Judaism teaches that God would much rather we did not go out of our way to test ourselves,[362] or try each other with suffering, nor relate to God as

---

[360] Proverbs 3:12
[361] *Talmud Bav'li, Shabbat* 55b
[362] *Talmud Bav'li, Sanhedrin* 107a

punisher and disciplinarian, but rather as teacher and friend: "Do you not know God? God is your closest kin!"[363]

However we might suffer, and for whatever reason, it can be an opportunity for growth, for self-transformation, for sensitivity attunement. We are here to learn, to self-actualize, and like any seed that is planted, we need to undergo fertilization in order to become organic, sometimes by the pleasantness of sunshine, sometimes by the mediocrity of rain, and sometime by the repulsiveness of manure. As the nineteenth-century Rabbi Shimshon Rafael Hirsch wrote:

> The evil which God at times seems to tolerate actually serves to discipline man by helping to strengthen his moral fiber and to ennoble him. The wrong which a man must endure is part of that training course of suffering which will refine him through discipline, a discipline to which God subjects only those who are capable of improvement and ennoblement.... Thus, we see that suffering is not reserved for the most wicked on earth....[364]

Then again, as a second-century rabbi once put it: "I prefer neither the suffering nor its reward."[365]

> Rabbi Shmu'el bar Nach'mani said in the name of Rabbi Yo'natan: "Tragedy befalls the world when the world wells-up with too much wickedness, and the first to suffer are often the righteous. For when permission is granted to the Destroyer, he does not discriminate between the guilty and the innocent, between the righteous and the wicked, and in fact he starts with the righteous." Hearing this, Rabbi Yo'sef wept and said: "It would then seem as if there is no [Divine] regard for the righteous and the innocent!" But Abbaye comforted him by quoting from the Book of Isaiah (57:1): "Thus are the righteous removed from having to endure the far worse evil that yet looms ahead."[366]

---

[363] *Midrash Tehilim* on Psalm 118:5
[364] *The Psalms*, Vol. 2, pp. 1670-169
[365] *Talmud Bav'li, Berachot* 5a
[366] *Talmud Bav'li, Baba Kama* 60a

Miriam Maron, BSN, RN, MA, PhD and Gershon Winkler, PhD

As human seedlings, we are planted on different soils of circumstance to effect varying fruition, each according to our particular constitution. Every person's disposition in life is therefore as distinct from that of the next as are their respective fingerprints, and so are their trials and tribulations.

The question, "Why do some wicked prosper and some righteous suffer"[367] supposes that life as we know it is the be-all and end-all. However, the discontentment that we might experience every now and then, whether we are naughty or good, and whether by our own failings or the erratic disharmony of life's circumstances, serves to remind us that this is not the place of paradise but rather the road *to* it, fraught with imperfection to allow for the attainment *of* perfection. And, when we overcome it, suffering demonstrates to us that the human spirit exists separate from and in spite of the limitations of the body and the physical reality in which it sojourns. Death, therefore, is not necessarily synonymous with suffering.

Ultimately, we might take solace in the faith that, if God designed a reality that allows for randomness, then that very randomness, too, is a part of the God-Will, and therefore one can find God even where God "isn't." And thus is God with us always, through every experience, although we can only *see* God when we look beyond the givens of circumstance; and all prayers, too, are answered, but not always in the illusory forms assigned to them by our subjective expectations and presumptions.

The Torah's proverbial Blessing-and-Curse package should therefore be understood beyond the common notion of Reward and Punishment. Rather, Blessing connotes the human experience of God's conspicuousness in life through the gifts of contentment and prosperity, of peace and well-being. Curse, on the other hand, implies the experience we have of God seeming absent or distant, such as in times of tragedy or when things aren't working out the way we want them to, personally, socially, or economically. When it feels like God is present and tending to our needs, as in "I will give you rain in its proper

---

[367] Jeremiah 12:1

time,"³⁶⁸ then we label it God's Blessing; and when it feels like God has abandoned us, as in "the heavens will shut up and there will be no rain and the earth will not give forth her yield,"³⁶⁹ then we label it God's Curse. Blessing, therefore, is when we experience what appears to be God cradling our welfare in the palm of the divine hand, so to speak, and Curse is when we experience what appears to be God having left us to fend for ourselves, placing us at the mercy of the unnegotiable laws of Nature, the whims of humankind and Random Probability.

In fact, the nineteenth-century Rabbi Shimshon Rafael Hirsch taught that the original Hebraic word used in the Torah for "curse" – ארור *arror* – is related to the biblical Hebrew word for "barren" or "bereft of" – ערירי *arriri*.³⁷⁰ Curse, then, implies barrenness, or a sense of absence – in this case the absence of Blessing. When Curse is in effect, then, it does not mean that God has withdrawn, only hidden, as in "I will hide My Face from them."³⁷¹ But, again, God only ***seems*** hidden from us when we hide from God,³⁷² as in the biblical story of the original "curse" of Adam and Eve. The Curse – the sense of God-Absence – did not take effect the moment Adam and Eve ate of the forbidden fruit but the moment they acted-out their own presumptions about the repercussions of their trespass by ***hiding*** from God.³⁷³ The concept of Curse, like that of the "wrath of God," is an imaginary reality map drawn by people, not God. It reflects the guilt and trepidation that humans experience when they misbehave, reinforced and overly dramatized by ideological and ritual dogma of organized religion. Like Martin Buber wrote: "One who rejects God is not struck down by lightning; one who chooses God does not find hidden treasures.

---

³⁶⁸ Deuteronomy 11:14-15
³⁶⁹ Deuteronomy 11:17
³⁷⁰ *The Pentateuch*, on Genesis 3:17; for example, Genesis 15:2 and Jeremiah 22:30
³⁷¹ Deuteronomy 32:20
³⁷² Isaiah 59:2
³⁷³ Genesis 3:8-10

Everything seems to remain just as it was. Obviously, God does not wish to dispense either medals or prison sentences."[374]

Sin, too, is not so much the transgression against the Divine Will or the failure to live up to what we are taught are God's expectations of us. Sin is not so much what we believe we have done against God – quite an arrogant assumption at best. Rather, sin is more about wronging ourselves and others; it is more about self-compromise, belittling ourselves for our vulnerabilities, apologizing to God for being human – sort of like Pinocchio apologizing to his inventor for being made of wood. When we hide from God, then, whether out of guilt or out of spite, God, in turn will appear to be hidden from us, for that then becomes our chosen template in the moment for our relationship with God and reflective of our choice of how we ***define*** that relationship. It becomes the cosmic choreography ***we*** create in our dance with God: "Is it I who hide My face from you? Rather, is it not you who hide your face from Me?"[375]

Nevertheless, even a casual reading of the biblical text would make one wonder whether the consequences of hiding from God far outweigh the benefits of its fulfillment; whether what we perceive as divine retribution is a more severe penalty to pay than banishment to the mercy of chance and circumstance. But closer examination of the history of both forms of consequence reveals the fallacy of such an assumption. As King David said to the prophet Gad: "I am deeply distressed; let us rather fall into the hands of God, for God's mercy is abundant, and into the hands of humankind let me not fall."[376] David realized that the laws and actions of mortals are as whimsical as those of the random probabilities of, say, a major earthquake, resulting in indiscriminate and unnegotiable catastrophe. God, however, bears no grudge, is void of the human emotions of hatred and vengeance[377] and executes judgment with the compassion of a loving parent or a dedicated

---

[374] From "What Are We to Do About the Ten Commandments?" published in *Israel and the World*, p. 85

[375] *Midrash Tehilim* on Psalm 13

[376] Second Samuel 24:14

[377] Jeremiah 3:12 and. 7:19; Hosea 11:8-9

teacher, deliberate and measured, purposeful and pedagogic.[378] The proverbial Covenant of God and Israel, in other words, was not just a form of security but a framework within which even **random** evil could become an opportunity for personal or national refinement rather than a meaningless experience of senseless tragedy.

It bears noting, however, that earthquakes and other "natural disasters" can of course be the result of human as well as divine action. Our planet, along with all of the stars and planets across our vast universe, is a living being, imbued with Soul higher than that of humans and a little lower than that of angels.[379] How we treat her, as well as how we treat one another and the creatures with whom we share our planet, can lead to a domino effect of "natural" consequences. More than once does the Torah warn of the capacity of the earth to literally "vomit" us out of the lands we inhabit due to wrongful conduct.[380] All of this is deep mystery and we must learn to accept that we cannot always know the reason behind every occurrence. It would be quite arrogant for us to assume we can pinpoint the "why" behind every happening. We can only **attempt** to understand, as human nature prompts us to try, but we must also know when to let go and just be in the mystery, and to remember that most of our questions are predicated on assumptions we ourselves have invented.

> The primary source of confusion in our search for the meaning of the universe as a whole, or even of its parts, is rooted in our mistaken assumption that all of existence is for our sake alone. For, if we examine our universe objectively, we will discover how very small a part of it we really are. The truth is, that all of humankind and all the species of life-forms on our earth are as nothing against the backdrop of vast ever-continuing cosmic existence.[381]

As God steps back from God-ing to allow us our space to be human, so must we step back from our human expectations and definitions

---

[378] Deuteronomy 8:5; Proverbs 3:12; *Talmud Bav'li, Berachot* 5a and 60b
[379] *Mishnah Torah, Hil'chot Y'sodei Hatorah* 3:9
[380] Leviticus 18:25-28 and 20:22; Deuteronomy 29:27
[381] *Mo'reh Ne'vuchim* 3:12

and presumptions to allow God the space to be God in our lives. This is the meaning of Covenanting, being engaged in a partnership that certainly has mutual benefits, but that is not solely dependent upon them or exacting of them, and which also retains ample room for each party to be themselves as fully as possible. And that means that every now and then, bad things happen to good people, "for so it arose in [God's] Thought."[382]

> "For my thoughts are not like your thoughts, and your ways are not like my ways," says God. "For as high as are the heavens from the earth, so high are my ways from your ways, my thoughts from your thoughts."[383]

The ancient sages tell us that when Moses reached the top of Mount Sinai to receive the Torah, he found God busily adding some finishing touches to the letters of the text. Days went by, ten, twenty, thirty…. Finally, as the fortieth day approached, Moses grew impatient and asked God what was taking so long.

"Oh. Sorry to keep you waiting, Moses. I've been busy adding all these cryptic interpretive codes and symbolisms to the text as delineated by a great teacher of Torah. His name is Akiva. He will walk the earth well over a thousand years from now, and he will render interpretations of the Torah that will baffle even *you*."

Moses rolled his eyes. "Really? Can I see him?"

God then instructed Moses to turn around, and when he did, he found himself way in the future, seated amid a sea of disciples who were gathered at the feet of the second-century Rabbi Akiva. Wow, Moses thought, listening with bated breath to the deep wisdom emanating from Akiva's lips, What a master. Admittedly, though, he could barely comprehend the lesson. "What exactly is he teaching about?" he asked one of the disciples. "Why, he's expounding upon the Torah of **Moses**!" replied the disciple. Moses was both dumbfounded and awestruck. He recognized none of it. He was about to purchase a copy of *Judaism*

---

[382] *Talmud Bav'li, Menachot* 29b
[383] Isaiah 55:8-9

The Invitation

for Dummies when God brought him back to the past atop the holy mountain.

"What do you think about Akiva ***now***?" asked God.

"What an amazing master!" Moses replied. "But I don't understand. Why give the Torah through ***me***, then? Why not through ***Akiva***?"

Said God: "Silence! For so it arose in [my] Thought."

"Okay, then," said Moses. "I would be curious to see what amazing ***destiny*** awaits him." And God showed Moses the end of Akiva's illustrious and inspirational life, crucified alive while two Roman soldiers slowly scraped him to death with steel combs. And Moses protested: "***What?! This is his Torah, and this is his reward????!!!!***"

And God replied: "Silence! For so it arose in [my] Thought."[384]

Commented the 18th-century mystic, Rabbi Nachmon of Breslav:

> All the confusion and questioning [which challenge faith, such as the paradox of a compassionate Creator of a world so filled with tragedy and evil] emanate from within the חלל הפנוי *Chalal Ha'pa'nuy*, the Vacant Void [empty even of the Divine Presence which otherwise fills all the universes; empty of God, so to speak, by virtue of God having constricted itself, absented itself, so to speak, in order to enable Creation to have the space it needs to become]. This void belongs to the realm of Stillness, Silence, as there is no reasoning and no words in that realm with which to respond [to these kinds of questions]. After all, Creation happened by the resonance of Word, of Speech, as is written: "By the word of God were the heavens made, and by the breath of his mouth did all the forces become manifest" (Psalms 33:6). And in Speech there is Wisdom, for the basics of Speech is only in breath, in what emerges from the mouth, and through them did all of Creation come into being. And it is like it is written: "You fashioned everything through great wisdom" (Psalms 104:24). And Speech represents the boundary of all things, for God boundaried his Wisdom within the [Hebrew] letters, that such-and-such letters become the boundaried space for this, and such-and-such letters become the boundaried space for that. But in the Vacant Void -- which

---

[384] *Talmud Bav'li, Menachot* 29b

surrounds the outer perimeters of the boundaried space of all of the universes [since all of Creation happened within the void, to begin with], and which is, in a manner of speaking, vacant of all [being beyond the boundaries of the Creation Space that occupies the rest of the void space] – there is no Speech whatsoever, and [therefore] no reasoning, [since it is] void of all the letters. And thus, all of the perplexity [about those unanswerable questions regarding the seeming unfairness of Life] that stems from there are in the category of Silence. Like we find regarding Moses, that when he asked God to explain the [justification for the horrific torture and] execution of Rabbi Akiva: "This is Torah, and this is its reward?!" – God's response was: "Silence. For thus did it arise before me in Thought," meaning, that you need to…not ask with expectations of response and explanation on this question. Because, the way it happened is the way it arose in Thought, which is on a higher plateau than Speech. Therefore…this is a matter relegated to the realm of "Arose in Thought," wherein there is no Speech with which to answer the question. And likewise is it with these questions and puzzlements that emanate from the *Chalal Ha'pa'nuy*, wherein there is neither Speech nor Reasoning. And… therein must one only have faith and remain silent. And therefore it is forbidden to enter that realm unless one is a צדיק *Tzadik* (an enlightened person), for then one takes on the consciousness of Moses, who is associated with Silence. Because Moses is about Silence, for he is in the category of what is called "heavy mouth" [slurred speech (Exodus 4:10)], of the realm of Silence, which is higher than that of Speech. And therefore the *Tzadik*, who is in the consciousness of Moses, the realm of Silence, can explore the words of the perplexed, for they, too, are associated with that place of Silence. And the *Tzadik* must only engage in such explorations for the sole purpose of lifting their souls out of the *Chalal Ha'pa'nuy* into which they have fallen.…And you should know, that it is through the ניגון *niggun* (wordless chant) of the *Tzadik*, who is in the consciousness of Moses, that he is able to lift up these souls from the faithlessness, skepticism, and disbelief of the *Chalal Ha'pa'nuy* that they fell into. Because, you should know that each and every Wisdom in the universe has its own very distinct song and *niggun*…and through each song a very particular Wisdom is conjured....And even the wisdom of faithlessness, skepticism and disbelief have each their own unique *niggun* and song that is associated exclusively with faithlessness and skepticism and disbelief.[385]

As a people, we went to our deaths over and over and over again, our final words absent of question and filled instead with the unfathomable meaning of "Thus it arose in [God's] Thought." Rather than "Why hast thou forsaken us?" our motto was "The seeming death of The Promise is the very contraction of its birth." Our dying words were *she'ma yisra'el, ado'nai elo'haynu; ado'nai echad*: "Hear, O Israel, Ado'nai is our God; Ado'nai is One,"[386] for which an alternative translation in times of doubt and dismay would go something like this: "Ado'nai our God hears, O Israel, [for in] Ado'nai [all of what to us appears as disjointed] is actually One."

The human impulse is a complicated one, as complicated as is the issue of Good vs. Evil. The Hebrew ancestors wrestled regularly with the question, and left us a sea of wisdom that steered clear of the convenient arena of duality and compartmentalization and attempted to instill instead an ounce or two of simple down-home emotional honesty. Good and Evil impulses, they reminded us, reside in each of us, and in the best and worst of us.[387]

> Observe the works of the Source of all Powers [*Elo'heem* אלהים], for who can make any sense out of what [*Elo'heem*] has seemingly distorted? On a good day, revel in [the gift of] its goodness; and on a bad day observe that this too, parallel to the other, is the work of *Elo'heem*; so [you see] no one can figure out any of it. Sometimes there will be a righteous person who is destroyed in spite of their righteousness, and sometimes the wicked will persevere in spite of their wickedness, so don't be too overly righteous...and don't be

---

[385] *Likutei MoHaRaN*, Ch. 64, paragraphs 2 and 4
[386] Deuteronomy 6:4
[387] *Talmud Bav'li, Sukah* 52a

too wicked...Rather, it is a good thing if you can hold on to **both** [qualities] without releasing your grip on either.[388]

This is such a profound and essential Judaic principle: that the potential for the highest good and the most holy of holies is made possible by virtue of the potential for the greatest evil and most profane of profanities -- that without shadow there is no light. "Thus says God, 'I form light and I create darkness; I make peace and I create evil; yes, I am God who makes all these possible.'"[389] Responding to his having been stricken with multitudes of diseases and other sufferings, the proverbial Jo'b [*Ee'yo'v* איוב in Hebrew] declared: "Shall I accept from God only what is Good, and not also then what is Bad?[390]

---

[388] Ecclesiastes 7:14-18
[389] Isaiah 45:7
[390] Job 2:10

CHAPTER THIRTEEN

The Kaddish

> There is a difference between a "name" and a "notion"…don't teach notions of God, teach the name of God. A notion describes, defines; a name evokes. A notion is derived from a generalization; a name is learned through acquaintance. A notion you can conceive; a name you call.[391]

At first glance, the traditional Aramaic prayer known as the קדיש *Kaddish* – literally: "Sanctification" -- appears totally irrelevant to the ritual of grieving, and completely unrelated to the scenario of death and dying in general, and one wonders why it has been for millennia considered so essential to the process of mourning that it is recited thrice daily for almost an entire year following a loss and thereafter every year on the anniversary of that loss. The prayer makes absolutely no mention of anything having to do with death and is primarily about the exaltation and magnification of what it calls "The Great Name" of God – the שמיה רבה *sh'may rabbah*. What name, in particular? No one knows. There is no mention of it. And for good reason, because God *has* no name in the sense of what we mortals define or understand about the usual meaning and implication of "name."

---

[391] Abraham Joshua Heschel, in *Moral Grandeur and Spiritual Audacity*, p. 162

What, then, *is* "The Great Name," and why is the *Kaddish*, this ritual of exalting it, so important in response to death? What is its relevance?

Our tradition teaches us that God is un-definable and therefore un-nameable. To name something is to define it, and God is total mystery. Any name we attribute to God is then little more than our finite mortal attempt at grasping at a particular quality of God which God chooses or has chosen to reveal of itself[392] or which we personally presume to know or experience. In essence, a name is a revelation of a particular aspect of someone or something but certainly not all of what that someone or something is. Calling a tree "Tree" is naming only that which we can fathom about it, which in turn becomes how we identify it. But the tree is far more than any of this. A tree is a physically-guised camouflage concealing infinite mystery barely described by anything we can possibly formulate. When the second-century Rabbi Akiva guided three of his most learned disciples into the shamanic journey known as פרדס *Par'des*, or "The Orchard," he warned them against any attempt at identifying or naming anything they saw or experienced during the journey. For *Par'des* has no tolerance for falsehood, and to name something, to attempt to identify something, is acceptable in the world as we know it, but not in *Par'des*. All that we name, label, identify is in essence far more than we can possibly conceive, and far beyond its external form and appearance, and a stroll through "The Orchard" will drive that lesson home quite intensely. Consequently, only Akiva emerged from *Par'des* unscathed.[393]

The "name" of God is thus un-pronounceable, because God is un-identifiable. The name of God is ungraspable, because God is infinite. Any name we attribute to God is in no way representative of all of who or what or how God is and veils more than what we can possibly fathom about God. When we make mention in the *Kaddish* prayer of *she'may rabbah*, the "Great Name," we are referring to all that God ever created, which – by virtue of emanating from God -- bears

---

[392] Exodus 6:3

[393] *Talmud Bav'li, Chagigah* 14b

The Invitation

God's Name, and is thus referred to as the "Great Name" in that it represents the overall cosmic way in which God unveils itself to us through our physical universe, through our earth, our solar system, and beyond – through **all** of creation. Every leaf, every blade of grass, every bird, fish, human, planet, molecule, is an integral part of the "Great Name." ***That*** is what "the Great Name" is all about.[394] It then follows that when someone dies, when one of God's Creations leaves, becomes absent from the very scenario of that which is the "Great Name," that the Great Name is then somewhat diminished by the dissipation of that particular Creation, of that particular person who, during their lifetime, had been a living piece of the Great Name. And so, upon their passing, we spend the entire first year of their death reciting the *Kaddish*, a prayer that is all about exalting, amplifying, basically ***reconstructing*** the now-missing aspect of the Great Name that once was personified by the deceased here in the Realm of Embodiment. It then becomes not only an honoring and restoration of the Great Name, but also of the deceased, of he or she who once embodied an integral part of the Great Name.

As the Great Name is restored, the individual who died on our earthly plane, and that part of God's Great Name that they took with them, become resettled in the Great Name that comprises the Realm of Spirit, which in turn restores the missing part of the Great Name which comprises the Realm of Embodiment, for "as above, so below."[395] And as the ancients taught: "Both Heaven and Earth are balanced by each other."[396]

The idea of the Great Name being representative of Creator's Presence within Creation is not just some exegetical theological homily spun by the early Kabbalists. Rather, it is clearly reflected in the very text of the *Kaddish* itself, where the primary subject is highlighted not as **God** but as "The Great **Name**," which is God's Presence and Intent breathing all into being and becoming across the Universe of Creation and beyond. It's all about "The ***Name*** of the Blessed Holy

---

[394] Zohar, Vol. 2, folio 124a
[395] *Talmud Bav'li, Pesachim* 50a
[396] *Midrash Bereisheet Rabbah* 1:15.

One," for all that represents the existence of Creation and the drama of Creation is enrobed within what is referred to as "The Great Name." And when someone dies, a part of the Great Name, a part of the scheme of Creation, a part of God's intent has been lost, so to speak, and we then pray for its restoration, for the restoration of "The Great Name" to the fullness it enjoyed while the person walked the Earth. In other words, their passing from the Realm of Embodiment has removed an aspect of The Great Name that was once them. And the belief that they now have transitioned to the Realm of Spirit – meaning that they still exist nonetheless – means that what has been lost here is now regained there, and whatever is added to that realm becomes in turn part of The Great Name in its flux across the length and breadth of our lives here.

And thus, nothing has been lost, and nothing is missing, and The Great Name, of God and of the personification of the Great Name as lived through the deceased, remain in-tact. The *Kaddish*, then, more than a rite of restoration of anything actually missing in the Godhead, is primarily for the benefit and comfort of the mourner, to remind them that the part of the Great Name that once was their loved one has not left, only transformed; that the Great Name remains restored and complete, and even more so than ever before:

The Kaddish

Yis'gadal ve'yis'kadash sh'may rabbah b'alma dee'vra kir'u'sey

May the Great Name be greater than ever and be sanctified across the universe created in accordance with Its will.

v'yam'leech mal'chusay b'cha'yay'chon uv'yo'may'chon uv'cha'yay d'chol bais yisro'el ba'aga'la u'veez'mahn ka'reev v'im'ru a'mayn

And may Its kingdom reign during your lifetime and in your days and in the lifetimes of the entire house of Israel, now -- within the spin of the wheel of time – and in a moment that is near; and let us declare our faith that it be so.

Y'hay sh'may rabbah m'vo'rach l'olam ul'ol'may ol'maya

May the Great Name be a Blessing-Source forever and ever and *beyond* ever.

Yis'bo'rach v'yish'ta'bach vyis'pa'ar v'yis'ro'mam v'yis'na'say v'yis'hadar v'yis'a'leh v'yis'halol sh'may d'kud'sha b'reech'hu l'ay'la meen kol bir'chasa v'shee'rasa tosh'be'chasa v'ne'che'masa da'amee'ron b'olmoh v'imru a'mayn.

May the Name of the Blessed Holy One be always a source of blessing and be lauded and be glorified and be exalted and be elevated and be honored and be raised and be praised far above all blessing and all song, all praise and all words of comfort spoken across the universe, and let us declare our faith that it be so.

Y'hay shloh'moh rabbah meen shemaya v'chayim olaynu v'al kol yisrael v'imru amayn

May there be Great Peace from the heavens, and Life, upon us and upon all of Israel, and let us declare our faith that it be so.

O'seh sha'lom bim'ro'mahv hu'ya'aseh sha'lom a'lay'nu v'ahl kol yis'ra'el v'ahl kol yo'sh'vay tay'vayl v'eem'ru a'mayn

Who makes peace in the Above Realms shall make peace on our behalf as well, and on behalf of all of Israel, and on behalf of all who dwell upon the Earth, and let us declare our faith that it be so.

Clearly, the subject of the *Kaddish*, as demonstrated by its wording, is none other than "The Great Name"; not the God***head***, so to speak, but the God***name***, the immanent Presence of Creator in the ever-unfolding drama of Creation. In traditional circles, God is therefore referred to as *Ha'Shem*, literally: "The Name," or *Ha'Shem Yis'bo'rach*, "The Name that is with Blessing." This mode of addressing or referring to God has long been an integral part of the Hebraic tradition, based on the humble acknowledgment that although God is unknowable, he makes himself known to us through the guise of all that is: "Blessing-Source is the Name, whose magnificence is forever, and whose grandeur fills the entire earth."[397] The guise of the Name is so effective as such that it takes effort and deliberation to remind ourselves that everything around us and within us is a part of that guise and thus a particular aspect of God revealed. In a way, it would seem that God's Name stands separate from God Itself, and even appears to have a life of its own, so to speak. After all, the world that comprises the "guise" is replete with tragedies that bespeak of forces emanating from sources far removed from anything remotely resembling what we suppose would be Divine Intent and Presence. The "guise" indeed does encompass both Good and Evil, in that it enables the possibility for the drama of either: "I am God, and there is no other, who forms light and creates darkness; who makes peace and creates evil; I am God who makes all of these possible."[398]

The seeming "separateness" of the Name of God from God Itself, of the Divine Presence from Divine Essence, is only in the eyes of the beholder, only in our subjective, mortal, finite perception and experience: "Let us praise the Name of God, for His Name *by itself* is exalted."[399] The messianic hope of the Jewish people is then that a time will come when "God and His Name will be One and the Same,"[400] when we will all recognize that Creator and Creation are One, that God Transcendent and God Immanent are One and the same; that the guise and whom the guise conceals are One, and therefore stands alone and by itself: "In that day, God *by Itself* shall be exalted."[401] The ritual of the *Kaddish* and its wisdom reminds the mourner that in essence there is no separation, neither of the Name of God from God, nor of Creation from Creator, nor of the mourner from the deceased; that all is bound up in the One Great Mystery behind all that was, is and will be, and who is at the same time immanent and transcendent, concealed and

---

[397] Psalms 72:19
[398] Isaiah 45:7
[399] Psalms 145:13
[400] Zechariah 14:9
[401] Isaiah 2:11 and 17

revealed.[402] In a similar manner, Life is representative of the revealed, the known, and Death is representative of the concealed, the unknown, while both comprise the same one fabric of ***Being***.

As Name is to God, Life is to Death. As Name is the veil of Spirit, Life is the veil of Death, for the very act of living is the very act of dying, as discussed in earlier chapters. The *Kaddish* awakens our consciousness to the Oneness of The Great Name and of The Great Mystery; to the Oneness of Life and of Death.

---

[402] Zohar, Vol. 1, folio 64b

CHAPTER FOURTEEN

The Four Sentinels of Night

> We exist not in order to be, but in order to
> dream the dream of God.[403]

In the biblical story of Joseph, he ends up in prison for a crime he did not commit, and there he interprets the dreams of his fellow inmates, both former ministers to the Pharaoh. When one of them is released he recounts to the Pharaoh how Joseph had interpreted the dreams of his cellmate and himself, interpretations that actually materialized as Joseph had described. In his recounting, the minister says: "And we dreamt a dream in the very same night, I and he."[404] In the tradition of the ancient rabbis, the narrative was understood not only in its literal form, they also saw beyond the context of the text deep into its heart and read "I and he" as a statement emanating from the depths of each person, that we and God together long to share the same dream, for we are both dreaming a dream in the very same night:[405] As we read in the Book of Psalms: "By day, God commands his grace [toward me], and at night, he sings with me."[406]

Life is a joint dream we dream together with the Creator as we journey across The Great Night. It is a journey of darkness illuminated only by moonlight and the star-studded sky, as in tidbits of enlightenment,

---

[403] Abraham Joshua Heschel in *Moral Grandeur and Spiritual Audacity*, p. 10
[404] Genesis 41:11
[405] See Rashi on *Talmud Bav'li, Shabbat* 133b
[406] Psalms 42:9

specks of radiance, and scattered sparks of clarity sparsely illuminating an otherwise obscure and befuddled reality. Like moonlight, all that we know is but a reflection of far deeper truths, and like the glitter of stars, the self-knowledge we seek eludes us by light years. No less than does the core of our earth burn fiercely with a brilliance surpassed only by the sun does the core of our ***being*** burn fiercely with a brilliance surpassed only by the Light of Genesis, the very wellspring of perpetuity. The Great Night challenges us to awaken the seeds of possibility that lay dormant deep within our consciousness; to kindle our inner light and fan it into flames of passion and awareness. The Great Night challenges us to defy its darkness and dance joyfully and brazenly in the face of its perpetual paradoxes. The Great Night is the drama of our lifetime, the arena of our existence in which we experience both struggle and respite; it is where we set up camp for the night while also preparing ourselves for the journey onward across the ford of the River יבק *Ya'vok*.

Ya'vok is the name of a river mentioned in the biblical story of the Hebrew ancestor Jacob, father of the Twelve Tribes of Israel. Ya'vok is the river this patriarch crossed together with his family during their journey back to the Land of Canaan following his lengthy exile in the Land of Aram. It is a crossing they made during the night after camping-out for a while. Centuries later, מעבר יבק *ma'avar ya'vok* -- "Ford of Ya'vok" -- was adopted as the title of Judaism's most comprehensive compendium on the rituals and observances around death and dying. A "ford," or *ma'avar*, literally: "That which enables crossing," is the most shallow and therefore most passable part of a river, and that is the area of the Ya'vok across which Jacob guided his family and their flocks during their night-time journey.

> And [Jacob] **camped-out** that **night**.... And he arose **during** the **Night** and took his two wives, and his two maid-servants, and he [himself] crossed over the ford of the Ya'vok [to make sure it was safe to cross. He then returned to the other side] and he took [all of his family] and brought them across the stream. And he then went back to retrieve and bring across his personal belongings. And [it was then that] Jacob remained alone. And [an angel appeared and

shape-shifted into the form of] a man [and] kicked-up-the-dust with him until the rise of the **Dawn**....And when [the angel] saw that he could not overpower [Jacob], he touched the vulnerable part of [Jacob's] thigh and disabled Jacob's thigh in the course of kicking-up-the-dust with him. And [still the angel could not free himself from Jacob's grip. And so he] said to [Jacob]: "Send me away, for the Dawn has risen." And [Jacob, realizing it was an angel] said to him: "I will not send you away unless you bless me." And [the angel] said to him: "What is your name?" And he said: "Jacob." And [the angel] said: "No longer will it thus be spoken, that your name is 'Jacob,' but rather 'Israel,' for you have striven with angels and mortals and have proven capable." ...And [Jacob] called that place פניאל *pe'nee'el*, Face of God, "For I have seen a Celestial Being face-to-face, and yet the embodiment of my soul was spared." And the **Sun** shone for him, and he is limping on his thigh [due to the injury which the angel inflicted]. And it is because of this that the Children of Israel will not eat the tendon of the nerve that is located in the vulnerable area of the thigh, to this very day, for [the angel] touched the vulnerable area of Jacob's thigh within the tendon of the nerve.[407]

Jacob's journey is a metaphor for **our** journey. Interestingly, he travels at night, alluding to The Great Night that is the scenario of our Lifetime. He does both during the night, camps-out and journeys-on, alluding to our experience of both respite and struggle in the course of our travels across the Great Night. He eventually arrives at the River Ya'vok. When we reach the Ya'vok, we stand face-to-face with our death, with the threshold over which we must cross to free ourselves of whatever might be holding us back, of whatever has been impeding our journey through the Great Night. Otherwise, our death loses its meaning because our **life** loses its meaning in that it is no longer **our** life but a life defined and determined by voices other than our own.

To live a meaningful death, our forward motion must not negate what we have left behind, but transform it. Yet, the danger in retrieving the past is that in so doing we might linger there long enough to sink

---

[407] Genesis 32:22-33

back into it. It is therefore important that we first bring all of whom we have become safely across the Ford of the Ya'vok, safely across the threshold of the passageway between the past and the future, between the known and the yet-unknown, and only then – once we've brought all of the pieces of our precious Self to the other side – only then might we go back across the Ya'vok to retrieve what we hope to transform. Just as Jacob went back to deal with his internal turmoil only after having safely delivered his family to the other side.

In the daring drama of transformative retrieval – what some might call "Soul Retrieval" – there is of course the risk or cost of "remaining alone" for a period, stepping into a very private and lonely struggle with one's Shadow-Self that feels akin to some other-worldly entity suddenly jumping us and attacking us from out of nowhere, from out of our "alone" place, forcing us into a fight, into a struggle during which we "kick up the dust" – as is the descriptive term used in the original Hebrew rendition of the story of Jacob wrestling with the angel, his Shadow-Self, the angel of his unresolved conflict with his brother Esau. Sometimes, when we dare to venture into the "aloneness" place, the angel of unresolved inner-conflict leaps at us from out of the long-forgotten void, long-buried memories and feelings which are then stirred-up as in "kicked-up dust" and a struggle ensues during which we are struck in our most vulnerable of places in the heart by the intensity of the angst of guilt or grief we had worked so hard over the years to bury as deep as possible in the void of oblivion.

Yet, it is not **Jacob** who finds the struggle insurmountable but the angel, and so he strikes Jacob at a very vulnerable place, the very part of his thigh that Jacob will need to continue on his journey, a painful blow which could threaten to **hinder** his journey. Still, Jacob does not cave-in. He is determined to reach a resolution, to make peace with his Shadow-Self, knowing full well that if he fails, he will only end up carrying old baggage with him into the new life that awaits him on the other side.

Jacob taught us to do what we can to hold on tight, to not cave-in, in spite of the pain, to not allow the pain of our realizations to incapacitate us, but to muster forth the strength of where we have arrived in the moment. After all, our Shadow-Self is still a shadow, and we still call the shots. Our Shadow-Self will try to hurt us with regret and guilt, and, failing at that, will try talking us out of taking the resolve to its conclusion with excuses like "Send me away, for the dawn has risen, a new life awaits you, a new dawn, so let go." But Jacob taught us to **not** let go, not just yet, not until our Shadow-Self can actually bring itself to see us in a whole other way than how it has seen us and judged us all this time.

When finally the angel of Jacob's Shadow-Self blesses him with a new name, a name that implies fortitude and ennoblement, thereby demonstrating its resolve to no longer shadow Jacob in ways that are negative or terrifying or deprecating, only then does Jacob cross over to the other side of his issues and reunite with his estranged brother Esau whom he had demonized in his heart for over two decades. And the next day, when he encounters Esau, not only do they embrace, but Jacob tells his brother "I have seen your face as if it were the face of God."[408] Jacob had succeeded in transforming the demonic into the angelic. In facing death, embracing death, crossing over to the other side of death, the man called "Jacob" birthed the man called "Israel."

Still, he limped. We never walk the same afterwards. Our gait changes; our pace changes.

It is important to note that the word in the original Hebrew narrative for "kicking up dust" is **ויאבק** *va'yay'aveyk* – "and kicked-up-dust" – which happens to be related at its root to the name of the river **יבק** *Ya'vok*. Indeed, a lot of dust is stirred-up in the act of retrieval while trying to cross over. The river itself has its shallow, passable areas for smooth, easy transition, but making the crossing with not only what we've become and achieved but as well with what we've left behind unresolved, could prove daunting and insurmountable.

Yet, when we endeavor to live a meaningful death, the journey across the dimness of The Great **Night** ultimately brings us to the emerging glow of the Great **Dawn** and the not-too-distant light of The Great **Day**. And while The Great Night is for grappling and enduring,

---

[408] Genesis 33:10

The Great Dawn is for hope and liberation, and The Great Day is for peace and resolve. And finally there is The Great Embrace, the healing and restoration. All four phases are highlighted in the story of Jacob and his all-night tryst with the angel.

"And he lodged that night in the camp. And he rose up in the night" represents the tango of respite and struggle that follows us through the Great Night of our lifetime, our complacency, our comfortable "settling down" into a groove that works for us, and the awakening within us in the middle of our contented state of self-acceptance of unwanted memories of past choices or experiences that had been left unresolved and long ago stored away in the foreboding attic of our subconscious self. And so we rise up out of our stupor and prepare to embark on yet another layer of leaving it all behind and pushing onward. But that only brought Jacob to the edge of the Ya'vok, not only in the meaning of Ya'vok as an impeding *river* but also as an impeding dust storm, as the memories along with all of the angst that they conjure are stirred-up once again, and so the struggle begins.

"Till the rise of the dawn" represents the breakthrough, the emergence from out of the shadows of the Shadow Self following the scuffle. The mustering forth of the courage to face ourselves fully, and to unveil all of what has been hidden away for the discomforting images they invoke about ourselves, let alone the negative judgments and critiques we harbor about ourselves.

"And the sun shone for him" represents the healing and clarity gifted from the dissipation of old judgment and guilt, of old blame and resignation, so that "none of it be left over into the morning."[409] Jacob emerges with a new name, a renewed sense of Selfhood. He can now embrace all of the parts of himself, including his Shadow-Self, and become whole. Jacob the follower of "whatever" has become Israel the warrior.

"And they embraced and they kissed and they wept...and Jacob said 'I have seen your face [in such a way that it is] as if [I were]

---

[409] Exodus 12:10

seeing the face of God; and I am reconciled."[410] This is the climactic phase of the journey and represents the reconnection of the parts that had been fragmented and the restoration of personal wholeness.

The four-fold evolution of consciousness in the drama of living a meaningful death along the journey of The Great Night is a major theme in ancient Jewish teachings. It begins with Abraham when the Creator gently slips him into a deep sleep at the onset of Night and informs him that:

> Your children shall be strangers in a land that is not theirs, and [the people of that land] shall work them and oppress them for four hundred years. And I shall also judge the people whom they will serve, and afterward they shall leave with a bountiful allotment. And you shall come to your ancestors in peace [and] be buried at a good satiated age. And the fourth generation [of your descendants] shall return here.[411]

"Your children shall be strangers in a land that is not theirs, and they shall work them and oppress them for four hundred years" alludes to the drama of Respite and Struggle, as the Israelites first enjoyed independent living in Egypt until a regime arose that enslaved them. **"And afterward they shall leave with a bountiful allotment"** alludes to the Breakthrough of hope and redemption. **"And you shall come to your ancestors in peace; be buried at a good satiated age"** alludes to the Healing of restoration and reconnection. **"And the fourth generation shall return here"** alludes to the Embrace, the reunification of that which had been separated, the consummative merging of fragments into the Oneness of their common origin.

In the ancient Judaic vernacular, what we customarily call "the Four Directions" are referred to as **ארבע רוחות** *ar'ba ru'chot*, Four "Winds." *Ru'chot* is plural for the word **רוח** *ru'ach*, which translates as Spirit, Breath, and Wind, as Wind emanates from Breath which in turn emanates from Spirit, from the Life Force within us, and – on a more

---

[410] Genesis 33:4 and 10
[411] Genesis 15:13-16

cosmic scale – from the Life Force that is the רוח אלהים חיים *ru'ach elo'heem cha'yim,* "Spirit of the Living God." Although each Wind represents a totally different direction, or pole (North, East, South and West), they are nonetheless essentially one and the same wind emanating from one and the same breath emanating from one and the same spirit, albeit operating in distinct ways and with distinct qualities.

The *ru'ach* of Life and of Death – although it functions differently in each realm – is likewise interwoven at its core, as interchangeable as is an inhale with an exhale. Judaism's fundamental belief in the possibility of resurrection, that in the end of times those who died will be restored to life, is rooted in this understanding and acknowledgment of the interweave of the *ru'ach* of both, Life and Death. As the Hebrew prophet Ezekiel was told by God to declare in conjuring life back into the bones of the slain: "Come forth, O one wind, from out of the four winds, and breathe into these slain ones so that they might live."[412]

What we call "living" is our dream of the Great Night, while what we call "dying" is our emergence from the Great Night across the Great Dawn of transition into the Great Day of Awakening. Resurrection is then not only about the restoration of the dead to Life but as much the restoration of the living to Death. Both comprise the entirety of a single day: "And it was evening and it was morning, One Day."[413]

The phases of our dream during The Great Night and the gradual evolution of our awakening are divided into four parts, also known as "The Four Sentinels of the Night":

> The night is divided into four sentinels. During the first watch, **Donkey** brays. During the second watch, **Dog** yelps. During the third watch, **Infant** suckles. During the fourth watch, **Woman** makes love [having been sensually roused from nursing her child].[414]

---

[412] Ezekiel 37:9
[413] Genesis 1:5
[414] *Talmud Bav'li, Berachot* 3a

These "watches," or shifts of Night, taught the 18th-century Rabbi Tzadok Ha'Kohain, represent the four phases of the exilic experience.[415] By "exilic" is not meant Israel's exile exclusively, but the exilic drama of each and every one of us, Israelite or not. We are all in exile, meaning on a journey that has taken us far from our origin and its unfathomable mystery and which continues to draw us farther and farther in time with every passing moment. Sort of like the Big Bang theory and that of the ever-expanding universe, perpetually fragmenting and floating away from its origin of Primeval Self. Yet, it is in the very act of expansion and distancing that we are actually narrowing our journey and drawing closer to the very essence of the very mystery that is our very Genesis. In the drama of falling, Moses taught us, we learn that we can fly, and are reassured by the Great Eagle that if we falter, he will catch us upon his wings, for he flies always just beneath us. The Great Eagle stirs our nest at times causing us to fall away, causing us to be exiled, yet follows us only a few feet below, its wings outstretched.[416] Likewise, does the Great Eagle catch us as we fall out of the womb into Life, and as well as we fall out of Life into Death.

All of Creation, inclusive of all beings, is in exile in that although Creator is integrally involved in Creation, our sense of the Divine Presence ranges pretty much from detached, uncertain and inconsistent, to erratic, random and flimsy. Nonetheless, even as we are exiled from Creator, Creator remains very much with us, just as God said to Jacob: "I will go down along with you into Egypt (exile), and I will also raise you up from there (redemption)."[417] In other words, that which separates us from itself remains nevertheless interconnected with us even through the separation, continuously weaving us with the thread of exile and redemption, of Life and Death, of separation and return. The severing of the umbilical cord in no way severs mother from child.

The Hebrew word for exile in fact reminds us that exile is not a negative but a positive, in that it moves us toward our unfolding. The

---

[415] *Tzidko't HaTzadik*, No. 22 and on
[416] Deuteronomy 32:11
[417] Genesis 46:4

word is **גלות** *ga'lut*, which happens to also be related to the word **גלה** *ga'leh*, which translates as "reveal," because the drama of exile – in both its agonies and ecstasies -- moves us toward the unraveling of our deepest Self and its endless possibilities of realization. In the struggle, we discover our power. In the seeming absence of God, we discover the actual presence of Self. The separation, the exile, is then an illusory experience at the same time that it is a harsh reality. As Life is an exile, so is Death a homecoming.

In the theater of Exile and Redemption, Phase One of the Great Night, or First Watch, is about endurance and waiting, thus Donkey, carrier of the "Time Capsule" that will one day fling open to reveal the Divine Intent that had lain dormant and concealed from the beginning of Time. Donkey then represents the knowing we harbor deep inside of us, the knowing that this can't be all that there is, and that there must be more to all of this than we can possibly grasp at this time and which will become revealed to us when the time is ripe or when *we* are ripe, whichever comes first.

Phase Two is about the approach of the Messianic era, which will be ushered in by Elijah the Prophet,[418] thus the sentinel of the Second Watch is Dog, as we've been taught: "When dogs are playfully yelping, it is a sign that Elijah the Prophet has arrived."[419] The relationship between Dog and the arrival of Elijah with news of the Redemption has to do with faithfulness, namely of the promise God made thousands of years ago, and in which we placed our trust through the millennia. Dog is faithful. Elijah's arrival will be a sign of the faithfulness of the promised Redemption.

Phase Three is about the **שכינה** *Shechinah* – the immanent In-Dwelling of God within Creation, also known in Jewish mystical tradition as *aima ila'ah* **אימא עלאה**, "Great Mother" -- reuniting with her long-lost, long-exiled children and returning them to her bosom. On a Jewish tribal level, it is about the Hebrew ancestral matriarch,

---

[418] Malachi 3:23
[419] *Talmud Bav'li, Baba Kama* 60b

Rachel, being comforted with the restoration of her children: "A voice is heard in Ramah, mourning and great weeping; Rachel weeps for her children, she refuses to be comforted, for her children are gone. Thus says YHWH, 'Refrain your voice from crying, and your eyes from tearing…for there is hope for your destiny…your children shall return to their borders'"[420] – thus, Infant Suckling at the breast of Mother, sentinel of the Third Watch. On a universal level, it is the Messianic Hope realized, when God will respond to us in ways that we can actually experience in our physical, emotional and spiritual embodiments.

Finally, Phase Four is about the sacred union between the *Shechinah* and God in which the Feminine, the *Shechinah*, makes the first move toward the consummation of her longing for her lover and heals her estrangement from the Masculine – thus, Woman making love. This is about the End of Times as we know them, as prophesized by the ancient Hebrew prophet Jeremiah: "How much longer will you meander about aimlessly, O the-daughter-who-wandered-away? For YHWH has created an entirely new phenomenon in the earth: the Feminine shall circumscribe the Masculine."[421] It is about the climax of the drama of the Soul's longing to reconnect with her God, Creation's reintegration within the bosom of Creator: "In that day shall YHWH be One and its name One."[422]

The sentinel of the First Watch of Night, Donkey, plays an essential role in the Hebrew biblical narrative. The mystery masters of old, whether the Midianite shaman, Bal'am, or the Hebrew ancestor, Abraham; whether the greatest of our prophets, Moses, or the least known of our prophets like the unnamed young prophet in First Kings 13 -- they are always described as traveling not by horse, not by chariot, not by camel, but by Donkey. Donkey is symbolic of the encounters and circumstances that move us along through our journey across The Great Night as well as the subtle force of Time which carries us from the womb to the grave. Donkey is the only other animal besides Snake

---

[420] Jeremiah 31:15-17
[421] Jeremiah 31:22
[422] Zechariah 14:9

described in the Hebrew Scriptures as being capable of speech. The speech of Snake enables it to seduce Adam and Eve into partaking of the Forbidden Fruit in the Garden of Eden;[423] the speech of Donkey enables it to protest against Bal'am's abuse.[424] Its capacity to speak, taught the ancient rabbis – what they called "Mouth of the Donkey" -- was believed to be among a number of unusual phenomena God prepared in sort of a time-release mode during the "Twilight" of the final cycle of Genesis.[425]

> The second-century Rabbi Shim'on bar Yo'chai elaborates on this teaching[426] and explains that the term "mouth of the donkey" refers to a deeply mystical concept, that at the beginning of time in the process of Genesis, Creator concealed the power of the Feminine – which is Timing of Expression and Fruition – deep within the Great Void. There, like seed within womb, this force waits for the right timing before emerging to coincide with the need for it within the Created Universe, the manifestation of which is embodied by the angelic being known as *Kam'ree'el*. And so, when the Torah recounts how God "opened the mouth of the donkey" in the story of Bil'ahm, it means that God opened the mouth of the Great Void to conjure forth the concealed force of the Feminine, which in this particular instance became the then timely need for the specific power of expression, for communication. This power was then integrated within the donkey by the angel *Kam'ree'el*, enabling the donkey to speak.[427]

The first watch, Donkey, represents then the concealment within the Force of the Feminine of what is to emerge when the timing is ripe. The final watch brings that journey full-circle as the Feminine emerges from its concealment to its revealment through its embodiment by Woman, who comes into her full power when she is awakened by the

---
[423] Genesis 3:1-6
[424] Numbers 22:26
[425] *Mishnah, Avot* 5:9
[426] Zohar, Vol. 3, folio 201b
[427] Rabbi Miriam Maron in *Ancient Moon Wisdom: The Kabbalistic Wheel of Astro Mystery and Its Relationship to the Human Experience*, p. 51

hungry cry of her child. And as she responds by gifting the child with both comfort and nurturance, she is further awakened, this time from within, as her passion is roused toward her lover. Her initial awakening is then from the child's yearning, and her second awakening – triggered by her **response** to the child – is her **own** yearning, the yearning for intimacy with her lover; the longing of the nurturer to be nurtured. She thus brings to the ensuing lovemaking the qualities of both passion and compassion. The Four Watches of the Great Night represent then a series of interconnecting paradigm shifts, of progressive causes and reactions, of kindling and flaming, in that the braying of Donkey awakens the barking of Dog which in turn awakens the hunger of Infant which awakens the nurturing of Woman which awakens her desire for her lover.

Perhaps this is the deeper underlying meaning behind the ancient Hebrew adage: "[When] Kindness and Truth intersect, Balance and Peace kiss."[428] Applied to the principle of the Four Sentinels of Night, it would read as follows: "When Donkey Braying and Dog Yelping intersect, Suckling Infant rouses Nursing Woman to kiss." **Donkey** carries the quality of Kindness -- חסד *chessed* in Hebrew -- as Donkey is about doing, enduring, carrying for other. **Dog** embodies the quality of Truth -- אמת *ehmet* in Hebrew – as Dog is about faithfulness. **Suckling Infant** carries the quality of Balance צדק *tzedek* in Hebrew – as nursing is about balance between nurturing and *being* nurtured. **Rousing Woman** in turn brings forth the quality of Peace – שלום *shalom* in Hebrew – as intimacy is about bonding. The Four Watches are then unified in the consummative act of the climactic kiss, in which the exchange of each within the other, breath within breath, wind within wind, spirit within spirit, creates "One Wind from out of the Four Winds."[429] Thus, Four Sentinels, One Night.

In our Life Journey across The Great Night, we strive to be compassionate and to be true; to nurture and to be nurtured – four essential and very basic qualities that guide us toward living a meaningful

---

[428] Psalms 85:11
[429] Ezekiel 37:9

death. Each of us is up for the challenge; it is only a matter of when. And as the first-century, **B.C.E.** Hillel the Elder used to say: "If not now, when?"[430]

> Rabbi Eliezer taught: "Turn your life around the day before your death."
> They asked: "But master does anyone know the day of their death?"
> Said he: "Exactly. Therefore, turn your life around today."[431]

---

[430] *Mishnah, Avot* 1:14
[431] *Talmud Bav'li, Shabbat* 153a

www.ingramcontent.com/pod-product-compliance
Lightning Source LLC
Chambersburg PA
CBHW020949230426

43666CB00005B/237